AN EXAMINATION OF WOMEN'S RIGHTS OF INHERITANCE IN NIGERIA, BOTSWANA, ZAMBIA AND GHANA

i

TABLE OF CASES

- *Adeseye v Taiwo* (1956) SCNLR 265.

- *Dawodu v Danmole* (1962) 1 ALL N.L.R 702

- *Gbadamosi Rabiu v Silifatu Abas* (1996) 7 SCNJ 53.

- *Mojekwu v Mojekwu* (1977) 7 N.W.L.R. (Pt 512) 283.

- *Muojekwu v Ejikeme* (2000) 5 N.W.L.R. (Pt 657) 402.

- *Nzekwu v Nzekwu* (1989) 2 N.W.L.R. (Pt 104) 373.

- *Nezianya v Okagbue* (1963) 1 ALL N.L.R. 352.

- *Osilaja v Osilaja* (1972) 10 S.C. 126.

- *Adeniyi v Adeniyi* (1972) 1 ALL N.L.R. 301.

- *Uke v Iro* (2001) 11 N.W.L.R. (Pt 723) 196.

- *Amadi V Nwosu (992)5 N.W.L.R 278*

- *Zaidan V Mohsons (1973) All N.L.R 86*

- *Udensi V Mogbo (1976) 7SCN*

- *Ahmadu Sidi V Abdulahi Sha'aban (1992) 4 NWLR.113.*

TABLE OF STATUTES

GHANA

- **WILLS ACT 1971.**
- **PROVISIONAL NATIONAL DEFENSE COUNCIL LAW**

ZAMBIA

- **INTESTATE SUCCESSION ACT NO. 5 OF ZAMBIA 1989.**

SOUTH AFRICA

- **CONSTITUTION OF THE REPUBLIC OF SOUTH AFRICA 1996**

UGANDA

- **CONSTITUTION OF REPUBLIC OF UGANDA 1995.**

NIGERIA

- 1999 Constitution of the Federal Republic of Nigeria Cap C23 laws of Federation of Nigeria 2004.
- Wills Amendment Act 1837
- Wills Amendment Act1852
- Wills(soldiers and sailors) Act 1918
- Wills Law, CAP 133, Laws of Western Nigeria.
- Wills Matrimonial causes Act, Cap.220 laws of the Federation of Nigeria 1990.

- Married Women's property Act 1882 Marriage Act

- Anambra State Administration and Succession (Estate of Deceased Persons) Law 1987.

- Administration of Estates Law 1991, *CAP 1Laws of Kwara State of Nigeria 1991.*

- Administration of Estates Law 1959, *CAP 3 Laws of Lagos State of Nigeria 1994.*

- Administration of Estates Law 1959, *CAP 1 Laws of Ondo State of Nigeria 1978.*

- Administration of Estates Law 1959, *CAP 1 Laws of Ogun State of Nigeria 1978.*

- Administration of Estates Law 1959, *CAP 1 Laws of Oyo State of Nigeria 1978.*

- African Charter on Human and People Rights (Ratification and Enforcement) Act

- *CAP A9 Laws of the Federation of Nigeria 2004.*

- *CAP 4 Laws of Anambra State of Nigeria 1987.*

- Gender and Equal Opportunities Law. No. 7 Imo State of Nigeria 2007.

- High Courts Law of Eastern Nigeria, *CAP 61 Laws of Eastern Nigeria 1963.*

- High Court Laws of Northern Nigeria *CAP 49 Laws of Northern Nigeria 1963.*

- High Court Laws of Kano, *CAP 57 Laws of Kano State of Nigeria 1991.*

- High Court of Kwara State, *CAP 67 Laws of Kwara State of Nigeria 1991.*

- High Court Law of Lagos State, *CAP 60 Laws of Lagos State of Nigeria 1994.*

- The Prohibition of Infringement of Widow's and Widower's Fundamental Rights Law No. 3 Enugu State of Nigeria 2001.

- Oyo State High Court Law, *CAP 46 Laws of Oyo State of Nigeria 1963.*

- Wills Law of Lagos State 1990, *CAP W2 Laws of Lagos State of Nigeria 2003.*

- Wills Edict of Oyo State, *CAP 63 Laws of Oyo State of Nigeria 1990.*

- Wills Law of Western Region 1958, *CAP 133 Laws of Western Region of Nigeria 1959.*

TABLE OF TREATIES

- United Nations Convention on the Elimination of all Forms of Discrimination against Women.
- African Charter on Human and Peoples Rights.

LIST OF ABBREVIATIONS

- AC: Appeal Cases
- ALL E.R.: All England Reports
- ALL NLR: All Nigeria Law Reports
- CAP: Chapter in an Act
- F.S.C.: Federal Supreme Court Cases
- FWLR: Federation Weekly Law Reports
- NLR: Nigeria Law Reports
- NCLR: Nigerian Constitutional Law Reports
- NMLR: Nigeria Monthly Law Reports
- NNLR: Northern Nigeria Law Reports
- NRNLR: Northern Region of Nigeria Law Reports
- NWLR: Nigerian Weekly Law Reports
- P: Probate Division
- S.C: Judgements of the Supreme Court.
- SCNJ: Supreme Court of Nigeria Judgements
- SCNLR: Supreme Court of Nigeria Law Reports
- WACA: West African Court of Appeal
- WNLR: Western Nigerian Law Reports.

TABLE OF CONTENTS

Cover Page

Table Of Cases   II

Table Of Statutes   III-V

Table Of Treaties   VI

List Of Abbreviations   VII

Table Of Contents   VIII

CHAPTER ONE: INTRODUCTION

1.0.0 Introduction   1

1.1.0 Background To The Study   4

1.2.0 Objectives Of The Study   5

1.3.0 Focus Of The Study   5

1.4.0 Scope Of The Study   6

CHAPTER TWO:

Laws And Practices Relating To Womens' Inheritance Rights In Nigeria: An Overview

2.0.0 Introductory Brief Of Nigeria Legal System   7

2.1. Inheritance- Law And Practice   8

2.2 Testate Inheritance/Succession   8

2.3 Intestate Inheritance-Eastern States   10

2.4 Intestate Inheritance-Western States (Including Mid

Western States)   13

CHAPTER THREE

3.0. Customary Laws Of Inheritance And Inequality Of Shares

    Among Women And Men   16

3.1.0 Igbo Customary Law Of Inheritance   18

3.1.1 Types Of Property To Be Inherited And Persons Who

    Can Inherit   19

 A) Lands And Houses   19

B) Economic Plants And Trees   20

C) Farm Produce   22

D) Money   23

3.1.2 Methods Of Distribution Of Property And Order Of

    Priority Of Inheritance Among Relations

23

3.2.   The Benin Customary Law Of Inheritance   24

3.2.1 Judicial Approach To Women's Rights And Concept

    Of Igi Ogbe   25

3.3 Yoruba Customary Law Of Inheritance   29

3.3.1 Method Of Distribution Of Property   30

3.4 Urhobos, Ijaws, Itsekiri And Isokos Inheritance Law   32

3.5 Islamic Law Of Inheritance   32

CHAPTER FOUR

Comparison Between Islamic Laws Of Inheritance And Other

Laws Of Inheritance.

4.0.0 Introduction ... 33

4.1 Differences And Similarities Between The Customary Laws Of Inheritance ... 33

4.1.1. Reasons For The Differences And Similarities Between Laws Of Inheritance

4.2 Women's Inheritance Rights In Some African Countries ... 37

4.2.1 Country Overview ... 39

A) Botswana ... 40

B) Zambia ... 41

C) Ghana ... 42

4.3 Specific Obstacles To Women's Inheritance Rights ... 44

A) Legal Obstacles ... 44

B) Political Obstacles ... 45

C) Socio-Cultural Obstacles ... 45

D) Economic Obstacles ... 45

E) Religion As An Obstacle ... 45

CHAPTER 5

5.0.0 Conclusion ... 46

5.1 Findings ... 47

5.2 Recommendations ... 51-56

Bibliography

CHAPTER ONE

1.0 INTRODUCTION

Gender issues are tropical throughout the world as there seems to be an increasing demand for more equitable treatment of women in all human actions. Many women throughout the world are campaigning, organizing and working together to improve their lives. Their aims, methods and interests are various.

Some are working on women's refugees, some are campaigning against pornography, some are demanding total legal equality with men, some want improved maternity leave, some are campaigning for abortion on request e.t.c. hence, there is no united women's movement.

However, they are all concern with improving the status and promoting the right and interest of women. These women's movements are usually described as "feminist". Alison Jaggar[1] identifies feminism as various social movements which are dedicated to ending the surbordination of women.

The feminist's claim is that women should have the same rights and freedom as men. In view of their various aims, methods, and interests, feminist theory is not uniform. Many writers have identified

---

[1] Cited by Bryson Valerie in Feminist Debates Issues of theory and political practices (palgrate New York 1999) page 5.

1

three main theories of feminist namely liberal, socialist and radical feminism.

The liberal approach is that women have as much right as men. The aim of the liberal approach is formal and sexual equality for women and men. Although the liberalism's claim for formal sexual equality for women and men has been successful and resulted in the acquisition of rights for women to be educated, to vote and to stand for political offices e.t.c. Some feminist disagree with the liberal approach because they feel that the approach recognises certain values that are mainly male.

Bryson[2] says the socialist theory of feminism like liberalism, promotes equal rights and opportunities to all individuals. However, unlike liberalism, it emphasizes economic and social rights and freedom from exploitation. Socialism allows women to recognise the ways in which men are also oppressed and to work with them to achieve a more equitable society in the interest of all.

The radical feminist's approach sees patriarchy as the oldest and most significant form of oppression for women. The radical view is that women are an oppressed group who has to struggle for their

---

[2] Bryson Valerie Op Cit page 16.

liberation against their male oppressors. Women must recognise that it is men who oppressed them and that politics has to be redefined to include family and personal relations.[3]

This study supports the socialist approach that women should work with men to achieve an equitable society in the interest of all: It is necessary that women should collaborate with men so as to enlighten the men about the injustice which inequality of the rights of men and women creates. The enlightenment of men in this regard could eventually eliminate the unpopular misconception of men that women are inferior.

Despite the differences in their approaches, the feminist's claim that women should have the same rights and freedom as men which has been largely considered in western societies has led to concerted efforts by international communities to hold conferences on the elimination of gender inequality. Consequently, many international instruments have been promulgated by the general assembly of the United Nations to address gender inequality. One important international instrument with regards to women's rights is the Convention on Elimination Of All Forms of Discrimination Against Women (CEDAW). CEDAW provides guidelines for legal policy and programme developments to promotes equality as a means of justice.[4]

---

[3] Ibid page 27.

[4] Kerr Joanna (ed) Ours by Rights: Women Rights as Human Rights (Zed Books London 1993) page 93.

Article 5 of the Convention Obligate state Parties to the Convention to take actions to modify custom and eliminate prejudices which are based on inferiority or superiority of either sexes or stereotyped roles for men and women.

According to Freeman[5], the examination of custom, the elimination of prejudices and development of measures to promote equality in practise as well as in law are the tools for justice.

Article 5 of the Convention is relevant to this research because the discriminatory laws which deals with the research examined are generally biased against women as they do not accord women equal rights with men as regards inheritance. Generally, under customary laws of the various ethnic groups in Nigeria, women are not allowed to inherit the estate of their late husbands and fathers. However, under some customary laws, women are given limited rights to inherit the estate of their husbands and fathers. The customary laws which deny women of their rights to inherit the estate of their husbands and fathers pose some challenges to women because of the death of the men. The widows and children are left destitute by surviving relations of the men who inherits the estate of the deceased.

---

[5] Freeman Marsha A: Women Development and Justice. Using the international Convention on Women's rights in Kerr(ed) ours by Right: Women's rights as Human Rights Op cit page 93.

The Islamic law on the other hand, allows women to inherit certain portions of the estate of their husbands and fathers. Many Muslim women are however denied this right by surviving relatives of their deceased husbands who prefer to apply customary laws of inheritance to the distribution of the property of the deceased Muslims.

From the foregoing , it can be seen that succession to property in Nigeria is governed on the one hand by the customary rules of succession ,the common law rules of intestacy and the states laws of Administration of Estate where the deceased died intestate and on the other hand , by the Wills Act or Law where the deceased died testate

1.1 BACKGROUND OF THE STUDY

Generally, most Nigerians both literates and illiterates are ignorant of the laws that regulates their private lives until they fall foul of such laws or there is a problem which affects their lives or the lives of their relatives as a result of the application of such laws. One area of law which many Nigerians are ignorant of or for which they have shown apathy is the law of inheritance.

Many Nigerians contract their marriages under customary law and so the customary laws of inheritance will be applied to the distribution of their estate after their death if they leave no valid will.

As stated earlier , many of the customary laws of inheritance deprive women of the right to inherit the estate of their deceased husband s and fathers. Some Nigerians are aware of the fact that if they die,their wives will not have the right to inherit their estate because of their customary law of inheritance . This category of Nigerians does not bother to question such laws probably due to their carefree attitude. Some believe that after their death, their relatives will take care of their wives , children and property.

Unfortunately, these apathy or carefree attitude to laws of inheritance which deprives women of the right to inherit the estates of their husbands has been creating problems for women. This is because in many instances ,their relatives whom their deceased husbands trusted while alive to take care of their children and properties sometimes convert the estates of the deceased to their own thereby leaving the widows and the children in destitute[6].

It is therefore necessary to awaken to the men folk to the unfairness of the laws of inheritance which do not entitle widows and their daughters to inherit the estates of their deceased husbands and fathers and the consequential hardship such women suffer.

1.2. OBJECTIVES OF THE STUDY

The legal and regulatory environment for Women's rights to inheritance is not sufficient and the few legislations that exist shows lack of commitment to gender equity in inheritance rights.

Also, the laws and practices governing inheritance and succession under customary law is very discriminatory and therefore

---

[6] Socioeconomic and legal right of women: the challenge Women Aid Collective (WACOL) Nigeria 2006) pg 5. WACOL is a non-governmental, non-profit making organization in Nigeria which is gender conscious working towards gender equality.

constitute a major obstacle to the achievement of equality between men and women. Even the Islamic system that appears to be the most just under customary law does not give equal rights to inheritance to daughters and wives. Social Justice demands that both forms of marriage should be given equal treatment, more so, when both marriages are recognized under the law as valid.

Nigerian government is a signatory to CEDAW and should keep to its signatory obligation as a state party. In particular, Section 2(f) which places an obligation on the government "to take all appropriate measures, including legislation, to modify or abolish existing laws, regulations, customs and practices which constitute discrimination against women" should be implemented. Similarly, the African Charter on Human Rights in Section 18(3) stipulates that " state shall ensure the elimination of every discriminatory against women and also ensure the protection of the rights of the woman and the child as stipulated in international declarations and Conventions".

1.3. FOCUS OF THE STUDY

In the discussion of the inheritance rights of women covered in this research, attention is focused on the status of women vis-à-vis their rights of inheritance in Nigeria.

The laws of inheritance covered by this research, attention is focused on the discriminatory aspect of the laws, that is to say, discriminations that exist on the type of property to be inherited and the person who are entitled to inherit the property.

In this connection, the research covers the following questions: Are women entitled to inherit the property of deceased male person and what are the rules of inheritance? Are there differences or similarities between inheritance laws under different customary law? How can these customary laws of inheritance be reformed to improve women's right of inheritance?

1.4. SCOPE OF THE STUDY

A discussion of the full range of inheritance rights of women Vis a Vis those who contracted statutory marriage and customary marriage.

Generally, a women's right to inherit depends on the type of marriage she contracted. There are two types that are recognized under the law: Statutory marriages and customary marriages, which include marriages under Islamic law.

Therefore, the discourse on women's inheritance rights in Nigeria in this research work is done in the light of diversity of legal system.

The study has criticized the customary laws which deprive women right to inherit to be unjust, inequitable and unconstitutional[7]. The study also compare women inheritance right in Nigeria with some other African countries.

---

[7]. Sec.42(1) of the 1999 Constitution of the federal Republic of Nigeria CAP C 23 laws of Federation of Nigeria 2004.

This study made notable recommendations to give women the right to inherit so as to improve the social and economic status of women, such recommendations were in fact aimed at the abolition of discriminatory laws so that women can enjoy the right from freedom from discriminations as guaranteed by the Constitution.

CHAPTER 2

**LAWS AND PRACTICES RELATING TO WOMEN'S'
INHERITANCE RIGHTS IN NIGERIA: AN OVERVIEW**

2.0 Introductory Brief on Nigeria Legal System

The Nigerian legal system can best be described as a hotchpotch of Nigerian legislation, English law, customary law (including Islamic law) and judicial precedents[8]. Nigerian legislation consists of statutes and subsidiary legislation. Statutes consist of Ordinances, Acts, Laws, Decrees and Edicts.

The judicature re-established under the Constitution is made up of Federal Courts and State Courts. The Federal Courts consist of the Supreme Court of Nigeria, the Court of Appeal and the Federal High Court. The State Courts include, High Courts, Sharia Court of Appeal and Customary Court of Appeal. The various states have, under applicable state laws, established magistrate courts and customary courts. Customary courts are the lowest in hierarchy of courts, manned by non-lawyers. Formerly, lawyers had no right of appearance in customary courts, but this has now changed. But in the customary court of appeal presided over by legal personnel, lawyers can make formal appearance.

---

[8] Joy Ezeilo, *"Genderizing the Judiciary in Commonwealth Africa"* a paper presented at an International Conference on Gendering the Millennium, 11 – 13 September, 1998, University of Dundee, U.K..

10

Being a federal state, all the three levels of government in Nigeria namely, federal, state and local government councils have powers to make laws. Whereas the federal law applies throughout the country, the state law is limited to the territorial jurisdiction of the state. A situation where each of the 36 states of Nigeria has power to make her own laws and to apply local customs within the state legal system which may vary from one geographical area to another within the same state, is nothing but complex.

The complex interaction of this multi-tiered legal structure which functions, simultaneously, in conjunction with very significant informal social controls based on gender, ethnicity and religion affects the status of women particularly in marriage.

The influence of received English law on customary law is very prominent in the area of personal laws (marriage and inheritance). Laws governing the marriage relationship in Nigeria tend to impact dramatically on women's legal position and status in many respects including domicile, property rights and legal competence.[9] Invariably, a woman's right to property depends on the type of marriage she contracted. There are two types that are recognized under the law: statutory marriages and customary marriages, which include marriages under Islamic law.

---

[9] Emiola A., *The Principles of African Customary Law* (Emiola Publishers, Ogbomoso, Nigeria, 1997) p. 122.

Therefore, any discourse on women's inheritance rights in Nigeria must be done in the light of diversity of the legal system.

2.1. Inheritance – Laws and Practice

Inheritance, which means the entry of living persons into the possession of a dead person's property[10] can be discussed under two major headings: -

(a) Inheritance under the General Law – Received English Law and local statutes (testate and intestate inheritance).

(b) Inheritance Under Customary Law (Wills and Intestate)

Basically, the law recognizes two kinds of disposition of property on death – testate and intestate inheritance. The rules respecting the latter are of greatest significance to Nigerian women.

2.2 Testate Inheritance/Succession

Nigerian law on testate inheritance/succession includes: The Wills Amendment Act, 1937 and the Wills Amendment Act, 1852, regarded as statutes of general application, which were in force in England on January 1, 1900. Also, the Wills (Soldiers and Sailors) Act, 1918 which deals with the formal validity of Wills.

---

[10] *Towards a Restatement of Nigerian Customary Laws*, published by the Federal Ministry of Justice, Lagos, Nigeria, 1991, p. 136. Nwogugu, E.I. *Family Law in Nigeria*, (Heinemann Educational Books Nigeria, 1990).

In some states of the federation of Nigeria, the Wills Law, CAP 133, Laws of Western Nigeria applies.[11] This 1958 law is essentially a re-enactment of the above mentioned laws on Wills. However, section 3(1) of the Wills Law, 1958 contains a provision not contained in the other Laws mentioned above to the effect that: "The real or personal estate which cannot be disposed by the applicable customary law cannot be disposed by will".

Further, testate inheritance in some states in Eastern Nigeria is governed by the Succession Law Edict, 1987.[12]

The provisions of part 4 of the 1987 Edict are similar to those in the Wills Act, 1832 and Wills Law, 1958. It is important to note that these laws apply in respect of the spouses of a statutory marriage and their children. No disability is placed on widows with regard to inheritance under a testamentary disposition. They are not treated differently from other beneficiaries with regard to their general right of inheritance as their counterparts in England. The provisions of these laws however, do not extend to widows who contracted customary law marriages.[13]

---

[11] These States are Western and Mid-Western States: Lagos, Oyo, Ogun, Ondo, Osun, Ekiti, Edo and Delta.

[12] The States are Anambra and Enugu States – two of the Igbo speaking states.

[13] Section 69. The Matrimonial Causes Act, Cap. 220 Laws of the Federation of Nigeria 1990, defines *"marriage"* for the purposes of the application of the Act to exclude marriage entered into according to Muslim rites or other customary law.The court held in <u>*Ahmadi v. Nwosu,*</u> [1992] 5 N.W.L.R. 278, that the Married Women's

2.3 Intestate Inheritance-Eastern States,

In general, section 36 of the Marriage Act governs the intestate inheritance/succession in the Eastern States, predominantly Igbo, for persons married under the Marriage Act.

The Act provides that:

(1) Where any person who is subject to customary law contracts a marriage in accordance with the provisions of this ordinance, and such person dies intestate, subsequently to the commencement of this ordinance, leaving a widow or husband, or any issue of such marriage; and also where any person who is the issue of any such marriage as aforesaid dies intestate subsequently to the commencement of this ordinance: The personal property of such intestate and also any real property of which they said intestate might have disposed by will, shall be distributed in accordance with the provisions of the law of

England relating to the distribution of personal estates of intestates, any customary law to the contrary notwithstanding; provided that:

Property Act 1882 (a statute of general application in Nigeria) is inapplicable to marriages contracted and governed by customary law.

(a). whereby the law of England any portion of the estate of such intestate would become a portion of the casual hereditary revenues of the crown, such portion shall be distributed in accordance with the provisions of customary law, and shall not become a portion of the said casual hereditary revenues; and

(b) Real property, the succession to which cannot by customary law be affected by testamentary disposition, shall descend in accordance with such provisions of such customary law, anything herein to the contrary notwithstanding.

(2) Before the registrar of marriages issues his certificate in the case of any intended marriage, either party to which is a person subject to customary law, he shall explain to both parties the effect of these provisions as to the succession to property as affected by marriage.

The Controversy

It has been very controversial whether the Marriage Act applies to other parts of Nigeria outside Lagos in view of section 36(3), which limits the application of the section to "the colony only". Some writers have interpreted this sub-section restrictively to mean the colony of

Lagos, which was the only part of Nigeria known during the colonial administration as a colony in the strict constitutional sense.[14]

According to them, if section 36 was intended to apply to the whole country, there would have been no need for the inclusion of sub-section (3) as the Marriage Act of which section 36 was but a part applied to Nigeria. In effect, there is still confusion with respect to intestate succession of persons married under the Act. In response to this problem, some states in the Eastern States namely Anambra, Enugu and Ebonyi States have adopted the Succession Law Edict. This legislation deals with inheritance/succession to real and personal estate on intestacy.

Section 120 of the Administration and Succession (Estate of Deceased Persons) Law, 1987 prescribed detailed rules of distribution of real and personal estate on intestacy:

> a) If the intestate leaves a husband or wife but no children, parents or brothers or sisters of the whole blood, the residuary estate shall be held on trust for the surviving spouse absolutely.
>
> However, where the surviving spouse is the wife and the intestate leaves brothers or sisters of the half blood, the

---

[14] Kasumu and Salacuse, *Nigerian Family Law*, (London: Butterworths, 1966), p. 262; (2) Obi, S.N.C., *Modern Family Law in Southern Nigeria*, (London: Sweet and Maxwell, 1966) p. 342 (3) Nwogugu E.I., *Family Law in Nigeria* op. cit., p.390.

wife's interest will be for her life or until she marries, whichever first occurs.

Thereafter, the residue of her interest shall go to the intestate's brothers and sisters absolutely in equal shares. The children of a deceased brother or sister will take the share to which his parent would have been entitled if alive.

b) Where the intestate leaves a husband or wife as well as children's children (whether or not he also leaves parents or brothers or children of brothers and sisters), the residuary estate shall be held on trust as to the value of one third thereof for the surviving spouse. The interest of such spouse shall be absolute in the case of a husband and in respect of a wife, for her life or until remarriage, whichever first occurs. The remainder of the estate together with any residue on the cesser of the wife's interest, shall be held on trust for the children in equal shares absolutely or failing children, on trust for the children of the intestate's children in equal shares absolutely.

c) If the intestate leaves a husband or wife as well as one or more of the following   a parent, a brother or sister of the whole blood or children of a brother or sister of the whole blood, but does not leave a child, two thirds of the residuary estate shall be held on trust for the surviving spouse. In the case of a husband, the interest shall be absolute while for a wife, it will last for her life or until her re-marriage, whichever first occurs. The remaining one-third of the estate together with any residue on cesser of the wife's interest shall be held on trust for the brothers of the whole blood in equal shares absolutely. In the absence of brothers of the whole blood or their children, the portion will be for parents absolutely.

d) Where the intestate leaves children or children of deceased children but no husband or wife, two thirds of the residue of the intestate's estate shall be held on trust for the children of the intestate equally. Of the remaining one third, one sixth shall be held on trust for the parents and the other one-sixth for brothers and sisters.

e) If the intestate leaves no husband or wife and no children or children of deceased children, but leaves both parents, two-thirds of the residuary estate of the intestate shall be held on trust for the parents in equal shares absolutely. The other one third shall be held on trust for brothers and sisters, if any, in equal shares absolutely. If no brothers and sisters survive, their share shall go to the parents.

f) Where the intestate leaves no husband or wife and no issue, but leaves one parent, two-thirds of the residuary of the intestate's estate shall be held on trust for the surviving father or mother. One third of the value of the estate will be held on trust for brothers and sisters in equal shares absolutely. If there are no brothers and sisters, their shares will go to the surviving father or mother.

g) If the intestate leaves no husband or wife and no issue and no parent, the residuary estate of the intestate shall be held on trust for the following persons living at the death of the intestate and in the following order and manner:

(i) First, upon trust for the full brothers and sisters of the intestate. But if no person takes an absolutely vested interest under such trusts, then

(ii) Secondly, on trust for the half-brothers and half sisters of the intestate. If no person takes an absolutely vested interest under such trusts, then

(iii) Thirdly, on trust for the grandparents of the intestate, in equal shares. If there is no member of this class, then

(iv) Fourthly, on trust for the uncles and aunts of the intestate but if no person takes an absolutely vested interest under such trust, then

(v) Fifthly, on trust for the uncles and aunts of the intestate.

h) In default of any person taking an absolute interest under the foregoing provisions, the residuary estate shall belong to the head of the family of which the deceased was a member. Such a head of family shall, out of the whole of the property devolving on him, provide for the dependants, whether kindred or not, of the intestate, and other persons for whom the intestate might reasonably have been expected to make provision.

2.4 Western States (including Mid-Western States)

The relevant law in regard to death intestate of a person married under the Marriage Act is the Administration of Estates Law 1959. It is important to note that, under the 1959 law, provisions of that law do not apply where the distribution, inheritance and succession of any estate is governed by customary law. This is because under the Administration of Estates Law 1959, the distribution of intestate estate applies only where persons are married in accordance with the Marriage Act.[15]

---

[15] The case of _Zaidan v. Mohsons_ [1973] All N.L.R. 86 illustrates these points.

According to section 49(5):

"Where any person who is subject to customary law contracts a marriage in accordance with the provisions of the Marriage Ordinance and such person dies intestate after the commencement of this law leaving a widow or husband or any issue of such marriage, any property of which the said intestate might have disposed by will shall be distributed in accordance with the provisions of this law, any customary law to the contrary notwithstanding provided that:

(a) Where by virtue of paragraph (f) of subsection (1) of this section the residuary estate would belong to the state as *bona vacantia,* such residuary estate shall be distributed in accordance with customary law and shall not belong to the state; and

(b) Any real property, the succession to which cannot by customary law be affected by testamentary disposition, shall descend in

---

Section 49 provides in detail for devolution of real and personal property on intestacy.

accordance with customary law, anything herein to the contrary notwithstanding."

There is need to observe that by specifically referring to marriages celebrated in accordance with the provisions of the Marriage Act, the law excludes monogamous marriages celebrated outside Nigeria and customary law marriages, whether contracted within or outside Nigeria.[16]

Law and Practice

With respect to intestate succession in Nigeria, there is a wide gap between law and practice. The existing laws with regard to intestacy of persons married under the Act are hardly enforced. The position in practice is that when a man dies intestate, the tendency or the usual practice in most Igbo– speaking states of Eastern Region is to subject all his estate–both realty and personally – to customary laws of intestate succession. Needless to say, these customary laws are very discriminatory against women.

The probate divisions of the High Court would hardly grant a woman alone letters of Administration. It must be jointly with the male children of over 21 years or a near male relative of the deceased husband

Testate Inheritance

---

[16] Nwogugu E.I., *Family Law in Nigeria*, op.cit., p.386.

Wills are not unknown under customary law in Nigeria. They can be oral – nuncupative wills or written wills. Customary written wills usually evoke controversy especially as to whether they must comply with the provisions of the Wills Act 1837 or Wills Law 1958 already mentioned. Again, there is also a problem of the exact effect of such a document.

Under the Maliki School of Moslem law applicable in Nigeria, a testator may dispose of part of his estate by Will. However, a Moslem testator can bequeath only one-third of his estate to persons other than those who would traditionally be his heir.[17] The remaining two-thirds devolve on his traditional heirs. There is also no requirement of writing or of signing and witnessing as in the case of statutory law. Professor Nwogugu is of the opinion that if the Will is in writing but does not comply with the requirements of the Wills Act, it would be treated as valid under customary law.[18]

Intestate Inheritance

Since customary laws and practices governing intestate inheritance vary from one ethnic group to another, it becomes necessary to discuss this topic in relation to three major ethnic groups in Nigeria: Igbo, Yoruba, Hausa (predominantly Islamic communities) in the next chapter.

---

[17] *Adesunbokan* v. *Yunusa* [1968] N.N.L.R. 79.
[18] Nwogugu, E.I. op.cit, pp.397 – 398.

CHAPTER THREE

3.0 CUSTOMARY LAWS OF INHERITANCE AND INEQUALITY OF SHARES AMONG WOMEN AND MEN

3.1 IGBO CUSTOMARY LAW OF INHERITANCE

In the vast majority of communities the family grouping is strictly patrilineal, inheritance is based on the principle of primogeniture, that is succession by the first son of the male line. The only exception of this rule exist in few matrilineal society of Afikpo or Ohafia where women have full capacity to own land (in so far as land can be owned by anyone in this area), and to transmit their right and interest to others either inter vivos or death[19]

Under the principle of succession in Igbo land succession is through the eldest son in the family who is known as "Okpala"

---

[19] Chubb,Ibo land Tenure, zaria,1943,para 41.

"Diokpala". In the case of nuclear family, succession is through the eldest male child of the deceased but where the deceased was a polygamist, with many sons from the several wives, the eldest son of each of the wives may take part in the sharing of the intestate. This is referred to Usekwu.[20]

In contrast, daughters and wives have no right of succession to their fathers or husbands movable and immovable property. Basically wives do not inherit because of the customary notion that woman are property and therefore object of inheritance themselves.

In <u>Nezianya</u> V <u>Okagbue</u>[21] , the Supreme Court, on the issue of whether the wife of the deceased member of a family could become the owner of her late husband real estate by virtue of long possession of the property which she occupied with the knowledge of the family or by adverse possession, held that;

> It will appear that the essence of the possession of the wife in such a case is that she occupies the property or deals with it as a recognized member of her husband family and not as a stranger, nor does she needs the express consent or permission of the family to occupy the property so long as the family made more objection to her occupation. From the evidence it is abundantly clear that a married woman after the death of her

---

[20] E.I Nwogugu, family law in Nigeria (1974) Heinemann Studies in Nigeria law p.406.
[21] (1963) 1 All N.L.R 352.

husband can never under native and custom be a stranger in her husband's property; and she could not at anytime acquire distinct possession of her own and oust the families right of ownership of the property. The Onitsha native law and custom postulates that a married woman on the death her husband without male issue, with the concurrence of her husband's family may deal with his (deceased) property. Her dealings, of course, must receive the consent of the family. The consent, it would appear maybe actual or implied from the circumstance of the case, but she cannot assume ownership of the property or alienate it. She cannot, by inflation of time, claim the property as her own. If the family does not give their consent, she cannot, it appear, deal with the property. She has, however, a right to occupy the building or part of it but this is subject to good behaviour.

The Supreme Court again after more than 20 years, has re affirmed the above decision in <u>Nzekwu V Nzekwu</u>[22] and maintained that the interest of the widow in the house is possessory and proprietary so that she cannot dispose of it.

---

[22] (1989) 2 NWLR (pt 104)373.

Daughters, like wives do no not inherit under Igbo Customary law[23] the only situation where a daughter can inherit is where, for example, she chooses to remain unmarried in her father's house with a view to raising children in her father's home. This is known as "Nrachi" or "Idegbe"[24] Institution. It usually happens when a deceased left behind a substantial estate, but no surviving sons or other male issue of the lineage to inherit. The idea behind this practice is to save the lineage from extinction. The daughter has an "Idegbe" or "Nrachi" is entitled to inherit both movable and immovable property of her deceased fathers estate. The legal interest vests in her until she gives birth to her own children. However, if she bears Sons and daughters, the son and not the daughter will succeed her in accordance with the rule of primogeniture.

Daughters also have no right of inheritance over their mothers landed property in a situation where a wife pre-deceased her husband, the sons will inherit and where there is no son, the husband inherits. If he is already dead his sons by other wife or his brother or his male relative will succeed in that other; But in those cases where deceased woman left daughters and sons, her daughter have a right of user for life or until marriage, over their mothers land.[25]

---

[23] E.I. Nwogugu,family law in Nigeria (1974) Heinemann Studies in Nigerian Law p.402.

[24] Ugbonna V Ibeneme (1967) F.N.L.R.251, Mojekwu V Mojekwu (1997) 7 NMLR (pt 215) p.283.

[25] S.N.C obi, Women's property and Succcession thereto in Modern Ibo law (Eastern Nigeria).

In some parts of Ibo land, the Oil-ekpe custom is practiced.[26] By this custom where the intestate died without sons, brothers or a father, his estate is inherited by his eldest nearest paternal male relation who is known as the "Oil Ekpe".

3.1.1 TYPES OF PROPERTY TO BE INHERITED AND PERSONS WHO CAN INHERIT

(A) Lands and Houses

Under the Igbo customary law, the eldest son inherits his father's compound exclusively in some Igbo Communities.[27] In practice, however, he gives part of the land to other sons at their request for building purposes. A man's compound is inherited by all his sons as a corporate body with the eldest son acting as a caretaker. In Ohafia Division, a man's compound is inherited by sons and daughters in joint tenancy. Where a man is not survived by any son, his compound is inherited by his eldest surviving brother of full blood. In the absence of a full brother, the compound is inherited by the deceased father. There are local variations with regard to the above practice. In Anambra, Ezzikwo and Mbaitoli/Ikeduru Divisions where a man is not survived by any son his compound is inherited by his father and in the absence of father, the deceased compound will be inherited by his eldest surviving brother of full blood.

---

[26] E.I Nwogugu,Ibid at p.407; Mojekwu V Mojekwu(supra);Udensi V Mogbo (1976) 7 S.C.I.

[27] Customary Law Manual. The communities are in Aguata, Idemili; Ihiala, Ogbaru which are Local Government Areas of Anambra State; Mbaitoli, Ikeduru, Orlu, Mbano, Oguta, Okigwe are in Imo State; Igbo Eze, Nsukka, Ezeogu are in Enugu State.

A man's land and houses other than his compound are inherited by his son or sons as a corporate body. In the absence of any surviving son, the land and house are inherited by the eldest full brother and, in the absence of full brothers, the land and houses are inherited by the deceased father.[28]

There are local variations with regard to this customary practice in some communities[29] where land and houses although inherited by the eldest son exclusively, the heir has an obligation to give part of lands and houses to the other sons for their residential and farming needs. However, the customary law manual does not specify a fixed portion which the eldest son has to give to his younger brother. Therefore, it appears that what the other sons of the deceased get is at the discretion of the eldest son.

It is evident from the foregoing that a deceased man's lands and houses are inherited mainly by his paternal relations. Where a man is not survived by sons, but by daughters only, the daughters generally do not have the right to inherit his compound or any of his other lands or houses.[30] There are however local variations in Ohafia Division where daughters in such a case inherit the deceased's compound, other lands and houses with the eldest brother of the deceased in control.[31]

---

[28] Ibid. Customary law manual page 100.
[29] Ibid. page 101. Enugu, and Igbo-Eze are in Enugu State; Nnewi is in Anambra State and Owerri is in Imo State.
[30] Ibid page 103.
[31] Ibid.page 103 Ohafia is in Abia State.

In Oraukwu town in Idemili Division, a daughter in respect of whom the *nrachi* ceremony has been performed inherits her father's compound, other lands and houses.

According to Customary Law Manual, *nrachi* is the practice whereby a daughter whose father has no male children is retained unmarried in the father's compound with a view to her having a male child in the father's name. If unmarried, she has the right to conceive a child for any man of her choice. The children she has are the children of her father whether the father is dead or alive.

B. Economic Plants and Trees

Customary Law of the Igbo permits separate ownership of land on the one hand and economic plants and trees growing on such land on the other hand. Thus, while the land itself is the property of another person, economic plants and trees growing on it are the property of another person or the community at large or vice versa.

Generally, a widow whether childless or not, does not inherit her husband's economic plants or trees and does not have the right to any share of these. Where a widow has sons, it is the son who inherit not herself though ,she may act as a caretaker for them if they are too young to take care of such property themselves, there are however local variations. In Arochukwu and Eme clans of Arochukwu division, a widow inherits her husband's economic plants and trees. In Ekiti division, a widow inherits her husband's economic plant and tree if, and only if the deceased husband is not survived by any son.[32]

In Mbano division, a widow whose husband is not survived by a son inherits the husband's economic trees and plants but subject to over all control of her and the property by the eldest nearest paternal male relation of the husband.

With respect to a daughter's right to inherit, a daughter generally does not have the right to inherit her father's economic plants or trees whether or not the deceased is survived by sons.[33]

There are local variations in Mbamisi, Enugu-uno and Ndeni clans of Aguata, Awgu division, Agulu in Njikoka division and Nkwerre division, the ceremony of nrachi may be performed where a man is survived by daughters and no son. After that ceremony, the daughter in respect of whom Nrachi is performed is treated as a son and will inherit her father estate including economic plants and trees. In Arochukwu and Eme communities Arochukwu division, a daughter inherit her father's economic plants and trees if the deceased is not survived by a son.

) FARM PRODUCE

According to customary law manual, the sons of a deceased man inherit his farm produce but the eldest son has a right to administer such property for his benefit and that of the other sons pending distribution.

---

[32] Ibid Customary Law manual page 112-113.Arochuckwu is in Abia state, Etiti is in Enugu State and Mbano is in Imo state.
[33] Ibid page 114.

There are local variations to this customary practice. In Aba Division, the eldest daughter of a deceased man as well as all the male relations who made financial contributions to the man's funeral ceremonies have a right to a share in his yams. In Bende, Ishielu, Northern Ngwa and Ogbaru Divisions, the eldest surviving son of a deceased man inherits his farm produce exclusively.[34] Similarly, in Enugu, Ezeike and Etteh clans of Igbo – Eze Division, the eldest son of the deceased takes the entire farm produce exclusively whether the family is monogamous or polygamous.

A widow generally does not inherit her husband's farm produce or any part of it whether the husband has surviving children or not. There are however local variations.[35] In Etiti Division, Umunumu and Akanu Ezeala communities in Mbano Division, a widow whose husband has no surviving sons inherits the husband's farm produce. In Oru Division, a widow inherits her husband's cassava and vegetables.

Generally, a daughter does not inherit her father's farm produce or any part of it.[36] Exceptions exist in Aba and Mbaitoli/Ikeduru Divisions. The eldest daughter has a right to a reasonable number of her father's yams. In Neke clan of Isi–Uzo Division, the eldest daughter is entitled to twenty seed yams or its value in money out of her father's estate.

D. Money

---

[34] Ibid Aba and Bende are in Abia State. Ogbaru is in Anambra state, Mbano and Oru are in Imo State.

[35] Ibid page 119.

[36] Ibid Aba is in Abia State, Ikeduru is in Imo State.

All sons as a body inherit the father's money. But in Afikpo and Edda clans in Afikpo Division, a man's money is inherited by his eldest uterine brother. In Mbaloye clan of Aguata Division, Enugu, Ezeike and Etteh clans of Igo – Eze Division Anaedo clan of Nnewi Division, Ogbaru Division the eldest son inherits the father's money exclusively.

Generally, daughters do not inherit their fathers' money.[37] There are variations of this general rule. In Arochukwu Division and Mbanesi clan of Nnewi Division, daughters inherit their father's money along with sons. In Ohafia Division a man's daughters inherit his money jointly with his sons and maternal relations (including the widow if married from outside). In the absence of maternal relations, daughters share such money with sons (according to seniority of age) and the mother (if married from outside the Division).

A widow does not inherit the husband's money. However, in Agudo and Ndeni clans of Aguata Division and in Ettiti and Mbano Divisions, a widow whose husband has no surviving son inherits her husband's money.

3.1.2 METHODS OF DISTRIBUTION OF PROPERTY AND ORDER OF PRIORITY OF INHERITANCE AMONG RELATIONS

It is evident from our discussion of the Igbo customary law of inheritance that many Igbo communities favour male children and

---

[37] Ibid. Customary law manual at pages 124-125

male relations like fathers and brothers more than daughters and other female relations like wives, mothers and sisters. Besides, the eldest male child is given preference over other male children. The variation in some communities where women as widows, wives, sisters and daughters are allowed to inherit and where male children are allowed to inherit property jointly irrespective of their seniority in their families are few.

In this connection, this customary law of inheritance is not only discriminatory against women but also against other sons of a man who, due to circumstances beyond their control were not born first in their families. This discrimination is not only unfair but also unconstitutional as it violates the provisions of the 1999 Constitution of the Federal Republic of Nigeria. [38]

There is no fixed ratio for the sharing of the property among the heirs. The share of the eldest son which is usually larger than that of any of his junior brothers is determined on the basis of what the administrators think reasonable considering the size of the estate and the number of the heirs.

The reason for giving the eldest son special right of inheritance and other male relations of a deceased man the right of inheritance as against his wife/wives and female children is that by the custom, the male heirs are under obligation to cater for the needs of the wife/wives and children of the deceased. While this reason could be plausible in the past when there were well established extended families, it is no

---

[38] Section 41(1) and (2) Constitution

longer so in modern times when the male heirs in many cases cater for members of their own nuclear families thereby neglecting their duties to the family of the deceased.

3.2 THE BENIN CUSTOMARY LAW OF INHERITANCE

There are two broad rules of inheritance under the Benin customary law depending on whether the deceased was a hereditary traditional title holder, a non hereditary traditional title holder and an ordinary person. According to the handbook,[39] the customary law of inheritance as regards the estate of a non-hereditary traditional title holder and an ordinary person is that the *Igiogbe* i.e. the house in which the deceased lived and died (and sometimes where he was buried) is inherited by the eldest son. However, custom enjoins the eldest son to accommodate his brothers and sisters provided they are of good behaviour until they are able to build their own houses and move out, or if women until they get married.

Other landed properties of the deceased are distributed among the other children according to *urho* in order of seniority i.e. according to the number of the wives of the deceased. Each wife with children forms an *urho*. Where the property is distributed according to u*rho*, the male children take preference over the female children. The eldest son who has inherited the *Igiogbe* is still entitled to a share in the other landed properties.

---

[39] Handbook on some Benin customs and usage.

Similarly, all other moveable properties are distributed among all the children starting with the eldest son. If the eldest child of the deceased person is a female, custom allows her with the consent of family elders and the other children to be given a reasonable share of the property on the ground that she is the most senior of the children. Where the deceased has one house with many rooms, custom allows the rooms to be shared among the children proportionately in order of seniority with the consent of the eldest son and family elders. This is allowed so as to unite the children.[40]

As regards inheritance of the property of a hereditary traditional title holder, the eldest surviving son is solely responsible for his burial ceremony though the other children may contribute to assist him. It is the eldest son who performs all the ceremonies. After the eldest son has performed the final burial ceremony, he succeeds to his father's traditional title and inherits all his property to the exclusion of the other children. Morally, custom expects him to give part of the property to his brothers and sisters. In addition, customs expects him to accommodate his other brothers and sisters provided they behave well towards him. Where there is no male child to succeed to the hereditary title, a brother or any male paternal relation of the deceased succeeds to the title after due confirmation by the Oba. The deceased's properties will be shared among his female children.[41]

3.2.1 JUDICIAL APPROACH TO WOMEN'S RIGHTS AND THE CONCEPT OF IGIOGBE

---

[40] Handbook on some Benin customs and usage. Op.cit page 11-13.
[41] Ibid page 15

There have been judicial decisions on women's right of inheritance as a wife or as a daughter under Igbo Customary law of some communities. In *Nezianya v. Okagbue*[42] and *Nzekwu v. Nzekwu*[43], the Supreme Court held that under Igbo customary law of Onitsha which does not give a wife the right to inherit the property of her deceased husband, a widow has the right only to occupy her deceased husband's property with the consent of her husband's family or subject to her good behaviour. She cannot lay claim to be the owner of the property or alienate it.

In view of the fact that the Supreme Court is the highest court in the country and its decisions are binding on all other courts, this decision of the court that a widow does not have the right of inheritance under Igbo customary law of Onitsha could impliedly mean that a widow does not have the right of inheritance under a customary law which does not give such a right to a widow. In *Mojekwu .v. Mojekwu*[44] and *Uke .v. Iro*[45] the Court of Appeal considered the legality of the customary law of Nnewi, which deprives a daughter of the right to inherit her deceased father's property against her rights guaranteed by the 1999 Constitution.[46] The court held that the *Olikpe* custom of Nnewi which deprives a daughter of right to inherit her deceased father's property or any customary law which discriminates against a woman is unconstitutional and is also

---

[42] (1963) 1 ALL N.L.R 352.
[43] (19890 2 NWLR (pt 104)373
[44] (1997) 7 NWLR (Pt 512) 283.
[45] (2001) 11 NWLR (pt 723)196.
[46] Section 41(1) 199 Constutution Of the Federal Republic of Nigeria Cap C 23 laws of federation of Nigeria 2004.

repugnant to natural justice, equity and good conscience and therefore unenforceable. Similarly, in *Muojekwu .v. Ejikeme*[47] the Court of Appeal held that the *nrachi* custom of Nnewi is repugnant to natural justice, equity and good conscience and unenforceable.

Therefore, a female child does not need the performance of *nrachi* ceremony on her to be entitled to inherit her deceased father's estate.

At this juncture, it is gratifying to state that the Imo State House of Assembly has enacted a law,[48] specifically to give women as wives and daughters the right of inheritance. The law provides thus:

Women and men shall have the right to inherit their parent's properties.

(a) A widow shall have the right to an equitable share in the inheritance of the property of her husband.

(b) A widow shall have the right to live in the matrimonial house provided she does not re-marry.[49]

The purpose of the law is to give effect to the elimination of all forms of discrimination and destruction against persons on the basis of sex as is presently obtainable in Imo State.[50] The law defines discrimination against women to mean any distinction, exclusion or restriction made on the basis of sex which has the effect or purpose of impairing or nullifying the recognition, enjoyment or exercise by women, irrespective of their marital status, on a basis of equality of

---

[47] (2000) 5 NWLR (pt 657) 402.
[48] Gender and equal opportunities law 2007 No 7 Imo state of Nigeria.
[49] Ibid Section 21.
[50] Ibid section 3.

men and women, of human rights and fundamental freedoms in the political, economic, social, cultural, civil or any other field.

Hence, section 4 (c) of the law specifically provides thus. 'Any existing laws, regulations, customs and practices which constitute discrimination against any person, shall be null and void and of no effect whatsoever and shall not be enforceable against any person'.

The effect of this section would appear to have abolished the discriminatory customary law of inheritance of the Igbo of Imo State that deprives women of the right of inheritance.

The Enugu State House of Assembly has also enacted a law[51] which accords women as wives the right of inheritance though daughters are not entitled to inherit. The law provides:

> Subject to the Marriage Act, Wills Law, Administration of Estates Law or indeed any customary law (not repugnant to natural justice, equity and good conscience) a widow/widower shall not be dispossessed upon the death of the husband/wife (of property acquired in the deceased husband's/wife's lifetime) without his/her consent.[52]

The law defines a widow thus: 'Any female person married under native law and custom or under the Marriage Act or any other law recognized in Nigeria, whose husband has died and has not re-married[53]

---

[51] The prohibition of infringement of widows and widowers fundamental right 2011. No 3 of Enugu state of Nigeria law.
[52] Ibid Section 4(2).
[53] Ibid Section 2.

This implies that women who married under both the customary law and the

Marriage Act are entitled to the rights of inheritance provided for under the law. To that extent, the law would seem to have abolished the customary law of inheritance of the Igbo of Enugu State which deprives wives of the right to inherit the property of their husbands.

While these laws of Imo and Enugu States are progressive, the pertinent questions are, are people particularly women aware of these recent laws giving rights of inheritance to women as wives and daughters? Secondly, how can women access these laws when the rights provided under these laws are violated?

Similarly, there have been many litigations concerning inheritance of *Igiogbe*. Thus, there have been many judicial pronouncements on the concept of *Igiogbe*. As stated in the preceding paragraph, *Igiogbe* is the principal house where a deceased Benin man lived and died. To the Benin people, the *Igiogbe* is not just a house. Traditionally, the *Igiogbe* houses the ancestral shrine and the staff of the particular family ancestors.

Osamuede and Okeaya-Inneh[54] said the Benin people regard the *Igiogbe* as the seat of the ancestors of the family where members of the family worship their ancestral god or deity. It is also the place where members of the family observe some customary activities like

---

[54] The Igiogbe controversies in the Bini Customary Law of succession: Judicial Review op.cit at page XI; Benin Native law and custom at a Glance (Gift-prints Associates Nigeria 2007).

traditional marriage ceremonies, naming ceremonies etc. This is why the *Igiogbe* in Benin custom is important.

It is clear from the discussion that Benin customary law of inheritance is based on primogeniture and *urho* rules that the custom places a premium on male children vis-à vis female children. The primogeniture rule of the past which prescribed that the eldest male surviving child of a deceased Benin man should inherit all his property to the exclusion of other children was very unfair. Hence, the *urho* rule was introduced to modify the primogeniture rule with its inherent injustice. By the *urho* rule, the children (both male and female) of a deceased Benin man who had more than one wife are entitled to share in the estate of their father as the property is shared among the children of the wives of the man.

Nevertheless, both the primogeniture and *urho* rules of inheritance are discriminatory against women. This is because although the *urho* rule allows female children to share in the property of their deceased father with the male children, precedence is given to male children of the stripes.

In the light of the foregoing, the Benin people who introduced *urho* rule of inheritance to modify the unjust primogeniture rule, should, in like manner, modify the whole of Benin customary law of inheritance to give female children of a deceased man equal right of inheritance with his male children. Similarly, wives should be allowed to inherit part of their husbands' estate. This will be in line with the provision of the 1999 Constitution of Nigeria which is the supreme law of the country.

In addition, the primogeniture rule which deprives other male children of the right to inherit the *Igiogbe* simply because they happened to have been born after the first male child is unfair and unconstitutional. It is unconstitutional because it violates the provision of section 42(2) of the 1999 Constitution which stipulates that no citizen of Nigeria should be subjected to any disability or deprivation merely by reason of the circumstances of his birth.

3.3   YORUBA CUSTOMARY LAW OF INHERITANCE

The customary law of inheritance of the Yoruba that the property of a person who died intestate is inherited by his surviving children has been confirmed by many judicial decisions. In <u>Adeseye V Taiwo</u>[55] the appellants as plaintiffs in the high court sought an order of court to join them in the scheme of distribution for equal shares with the defendants (defendants)in the proceeds of sale of a property. The appellants claimed to be blood relations of chief Taiwo deceased's mother's sister. The respondents were the daughters and grand children of the deceased. The appellants claim was dismissed on the ground that the only children of the children of the deceased could succeed to his estate. The appellants appealed to the federal Supreme court. Therefore the issue for the determination was whether blood relations of a deceased Yoruba person, who was survived by children, could have a share of his real property under the native law and custom of the Yoruba. the federal supreme court held that the children of a deceased person could inherit his real property to the exclusion of

---

[55] (1956), SCNLR 265, <u>Gbadamosi Rafiu V Silifatu Abasi</u>(1996) 7 SCNJ 53 at page 55.

other blood relations. The Court stated thus; "under the native of the Yorubas the real property of the deceased person who had children surviving goes to his children and not to his uncles, aunty and cousin".

The landed property of a deceased person is inherited jointly by his children as family property with the eldest son surviving him as the head of the family called Dawodu. Landed property inherited by the children of the deceased his family property could be a house where the deceased lived during his lifetime. It pertinent to state it is not necessary that the deceased expressly provide that his landed property should be used as a family property.

This is because it is an establish rule of Yoruba customary law of inheritance that on the death of a person intestate his landed property automatically devolves to his immediate family (i.e. children) as family property.

3.3.1 METHOD OF DISTRIBUTION OF PROPERTY

There are two methods of distributing a deceased self-acquired property (other than that reserved as family property) under Yoruba customary law of inheritance. The two methods are called *Idi-Igi* (per stripe) and *Ori Ojori* (per capita). The *Idi-Igi* (per stripe) method is generally used where a deceased man had more than one wife. The property is divided into equal shares in accordance with the number of the wives of the deceased with children. Each mother with children or a child forms a branch of the family or a stripe for the purpose of inheritance. The children of each wife take a share regardless of how many they are. The children of each wife then divide their share as they like among themselves. However, where the deceased had only one wife, his property is distributed equally among his children.

The second method is *Ori Ojori* i.e. distribution per capita. By this method, the distribution of the property among the children is equal. The difference between the two methods is that all the children get equal share under *Ori Ojori* (Per capita) while under *Idi-Igi* method, though the stripes get equal shares, the share of each child depends on the number of the children in each stripe. *Idi-Igi* (per stripe) method generally appears unfair because the number of children born by each wife is not considered. Hence, under that method, an only child of one mother has an equal share with many children of another mother. This method is inequitable. On the other hand, the equal treatment of all children under *Ori Ojori* (per capita) method is fair and equitable. This may also prevent dispute and envy in the family and preserve unity among the children.

An attempt made in the case of <u>Dawodu v. Danmole</u>[56] to get the court to declare *Idi-Igi* (per stripe) method as repugnant to the principle of natural justice, equity and good conscience did not succeed. In that case, the plaintiff/respondent claimed that the rents from the property of their deceased father who had four wives should be divided according to *Idi-Igi* (per stripe) method. Therefore the property should be divided into four parts according to the number of wives of the deceased with children. The defendants/appellants claimed that *Ori-Ojori* (per capita) method should be used to distribute

---

[56] (1962) 1 ALL NLR 702; <u>Adeniyi V Adeniyi</u> (1972) I ALL NLR 301.

the rents so that the rents should be divided into nine parts according to the number of the children of the deceased. The defendants/appellants also claimed that the *Idi-Igi* (per stripe) method of distribution had been abrogated and that the new method was the *Ori Ojori* (per capita) method.

The trial court held that the *Idi-Igi* (per stripe) method of distribution of property had not been abrogated but held that the custom was repugnant to natural justice, equity and good conscience because it was contrary to the modern idea of basis for distribution which is the number of the children of an intestate. He therefore ordered the division of the rents into nine parts. On appeal, the Federal Supreme Court held that the relevant customary law was *Idi-Igi* (per stripe) and that the customary law was not contrary to natural justice, equity and good conscience.

Surviving wives of deceased persons who died intestate are not entitled to inherit the property of their deceased husbands. There have been judicial pronouncements on this customary rule. In <u>Osilaja v. Osilaja</u>[57], the Supreme Court held that the rule that a widow cannot inherit her deceased husband property has become so notorious by frequent proof in court and has become judicially noticed.

3.4 URHOBOS, IJAWS, ITSEKIRI AND ISOKOS INHERITANCE LAW

The Urhobos, Ijaws, Itesekiri and Isokos of Delta state have similar rules of inheritance. Both male and female children are entitled

---

[57] (1972) 10 SC 126.

to inherit from their father's estate. The eldest son must as of right inherit the house in which his deceased father lived whilst he was alive. If a man has many wives whilst he was alive, the per stripes method is often referred. In the case of <u>Thomson oke and Anor V Robinson oke</u> and Anor[58] the Supreme Court upheld the decision of the high court that under Urhobos and Itskiri customary law of succession, it is the eldest son that inherits the house where his deceased father lived and died. Also the wife or wives of a deceased Urhobo man are part of his property to be inherited[59] and are therefore not entitled to the deceased estate. However, the widow has a right of choice either to remarry or not to remarry, if she refuses to remarry, and she cannot be compelled by the family of her deceased husband to do so.

3.5 ISLAMIC LAW OF INHERITANCE

Succession rights under Islamic law are mathematically laid out in the Quar'an. Under the law, wives and daughters are entitled to participate in the sharing of the estate of their deceased husband or father. When there are children or other descendants, the widows portion is one-eight of the deceased estate. If there are more than one widow, the one-eight is shared equally amongst them. A woman without any child inherits one – quarter of the deceased husband's estate. The following are the primary heirs and their shares:

a) Father, one-sixth (1/6)

---

[58] *Ahmadu Sidi v. Abdulahi Sha'aban* [1992] 4 NWLR p. 113.
[59] Quar'an Chp. 4 verse 14, see Professor Yakubu *"Property Inheritance and Distribution of Estates under Customary Law"* in *Towards A Restatement of Nigerian Customary Laws* op. cit. pp. 144 – 145.

b) Grandfather, one-sixth (1/6)

c) Mother, one-sixth (1/6) with a child and one-third (1/3) without a child.

d) Grandmother, one-sixth (1/6) with a child and one-third (1/3) without a child.

e) Husband, one-fourth (1/4) with a child and one-half (1/2) without a child.

f) Wife or wives, one-eighth (1/8) with a child and one-fourth (1/4) without a child.

g) Daughter, half (1/2) when alone, and two-third (2/3) if more than one son.

h) Son's daughter, howsoever like above.

i) Uterine brother or sister, one-sixth (1/6) if one, one-third (1/3) if more.

j) Full sister, one-sixth (1/6) when alone, and two-third (2/3) if more.

k) Consanguine sister, half (1/2) if one and two third (2/3) if more.

CHAPTER 4

COMPARISON BETWEEN ISLAMIC LAWS OF INHERITANCE AND OTHER LAWS OF INHERITANCE

4.0.0 INTRODUCTION

Having discussed the Islamic law of inheritance and other laws of inheritance in the preceding chapters, it is appropriate to examine the differences and similarities between the laws.

In this connection, this chapter examines the differences and similarities, between the Islamic law and customary laws of inheritance. The rationale for the differences and similarities are also discussed.

4.1 DIFFERENCES AND SIMILARITIES BETWEEN THE CUSTOMARY LAWS OF INHERITANCE.

Under the Igbo and Benin Customary Laws of Inheritance, the rule of primogeniture (inheritance by the eldest surviving son of a deceased to the exclusion of all other heirs) applies to inheritance of the main dwelling house of a deceased man. The eldest surviving son of a deceased Igbo or Benin is entitled to inherit his father's main dwelling house (called *Obi* among the Igbo's and *igiogbe* among the Benin's) to the exclusion of all other children of the deceased. There are local variations among some Igbo communities where the *obi* is inherited jointly by all the sons of a deceased person as a corporate body. Moreover, in the distribution of other properties the eldest son is given preference over the other sons.

Islamic Law of inheritance does not recognize the rule of primogeniture. Hausa and Fulani law does not regard any property as special to be inherited only by the eldest son. All sons of a deceased person have equal rights to all the property of the deceased. The eldest son of a deceased is not given preference in the distribution of the property simply because he was opportune to have been the first son of the family.

As discussed in the preceding chapter, an established rule of Yoruba Customary Law of Inheritance is that on the death of a person intestate, his landed property automatically devolves on his children as family property until it is partitioned with the consent of all members of the family (children). The eldest son as the head of the family manages the family's property for the benefit of all members. No member of the family or heir can alienate or dispose of family property which has not been partitioned without the consent of all other members of the family.

The concept of family property as it is under Yoruba Customary Law is not recognized by Hausas and Fulani's. In contrast, under Islamic Law, landed property of a deceased is shared among his children and other heirs in the proportion specified by the law. Each heir has a right to deal with his own share of the property as he wishes.

Generally, under Igbo Customary Law, a daughter does not have the right to inherit the landed property of her deceased's father. There are however local variations in Ohafia Division of Abia State where a daughter can inherit her deceased father's landed property if the father has no son. In some other communities a daughter in respect of whom the *nrachi* ceremony has been performed inherits her father's landed property. These exceptions are however few and insignificant.

Under the Benin Customary Law, daughters have the rights to inherit their father's landed property apart from the *igiogbe* when the property is distributed. However sons are given preference over daughters in the distribution of the property. Although a daughter who is the eldest child of a deceased person under the Benin customary law of inheritance does not have the right to inherit the *igiogbe,* the custom allows her to be given a reasonable share of the other property of her father by the mutual agreement of the family elders and the other children. The fact that it is the elders and other children who determine whether or not she should be given a reasonable share and what amounts to a reasonable share means that what she gets as the eldest child is not of right. It depends entirely on the whims and caprices of the elders of the family and the other children. Thus, the custom is unjust and discriminatory.

On the other hand, under Islamic Law, a daughter has a right like a son to inherit her father's property both landed and personal. This is because there is no distinction between landed and personal property. Under Islamic Law, all persons who are entitled to inheritance inherit all types of the property of a deceased person.

The shares of daughters under the customary laws of inheritance of the Yoruba, Benin and the Igbo communities where daughters have the right to inherit their father's property are not fixed. In contrast, under Islamic Law, the shares of daughters in the property of their parents are fixed in the Holy Quran. In fact, the shares of sons and daughters in the property of their parents are fixed by Allah in the Holy Quran.[60] While Yoruba customary law gives a daughter equal share with a son in the property of their deceased parents, Islamic law gives a daughter half of the share of a son where a deceased is survived by daughters and sons.

Under the Igbo, Benin and Yoruba customary laws of inheritance, wives do not have the right to inherit the property of their deceased husbands. The exceptions to this rule among some Igbo communities of Arochukwu, Etiti and Mbano[61] where widows have the right to inherit certain property of their husbands are few and insignificant. Islamic law on the other hand gives wives the right to inherit the property of their deceased husbands. The share of a wife in the property of her late husband is also fixed by Allah in the Holy Quran[62].

There is no similarity between Islamic law of inheritance, the Igbo and Benin customary laws of inheritance. However, there is a striking similarity between Islamic Law of inheritance and Yoruba customary law of inheritance. Both laws give daughters and sons the rights to inherit both landed and personal property of their parents.

Therefore, both laws do not distinguish between landed and personal properties to be inherited by persons who are entitled to inherit the properties

---

[60] Quran Chapter 4 verse 11.
[61] Customary law manual Op cit. pages 112-113. Arochukwu is in Abia state. Etiti is in Enugu and Mbano is in Imo State.
[62] Quran Chapter 4 verse 12.

4.1.1. REASONS FOR THE DIFFERENCES AND SIMILARITIES BETWEEN LAWS OF INHERITANCE

The rationale for allowing the eldest son to inherit the main dwelling house of his deceased father under the Igbo and Benin customary laws of inheritance instead of a daughter, who is the eldest surviving child, is that the eldest surviving son of a man succeeds to his father's status as the head of his immediate family. As the head of his father's immediate family, he has a duty to provide for the wives and children of his late father until the children are of age to fend for themselves[63] While this reason could be plausible in the past when the extended family system was operating well, with the disintegration of the extended family system nowadays, many male heirs are now concerned with the care of their own nuclear families. Thus, they neglect their duties to cater for the wives and children of their deceased father.

Moreover, under the Benin customary law, the rationale for inheritance of the *igiogbe* by the eldest son is because the *igiogbe* is regarded by the Benin people as a special house where the ancestral god and ancestral staff of the family are kept.

The *igiogbe* is also the place where the ancestral god is worshipped. It is the eldest son who has the duty to take charge of both the ancestral shrine and staff. Osamuede[64] says under the Benin

---

[63] Onokan Margaret Chinyere, Op.Cit Page 342 Osamuede Efe Sophia Op.cit pp 22-23. Nwabueze B.O Nigeria land law (Nwamife Nigeria 1972) p.393.
[64] Osamuede Efe Sophia OP.cit pp 27-28.

customary law, a woman cannot be in charge of the ancestral shrine and staff.

It is deducible that this is the reason for preventing a daughter who is the eldest child of a deceased Benin man from inheriting his *igiogbe*. Granted that a daughter who is the eldest child is disallowed from inheriting the *igiogbe* because she is considered incapable of taking charge of the ancestral shrine, it is only fair that she should be compensated by giving her preference over the other children in the distribution of the other properties of her father. The present custom where the eldest son and other sons are given preference over a daughter who is the eldest child and other daughters in the distribution of other properties is unjust and discriminatory.

The rationale behind the general rule that a daughter does not have the right to inherit the landed property of her deceased father under Igbo customary law is because the people believed that landed property should remain in the family of the founder or owner. In view of the fact that a daughter is expected to get married and eventually leave her parents' home to the family of her husband, she is denied the right to inherit her father's landed property because after her marriage, the landed property will become that of her husband.

This study feels that this reason is not cogent enough. Notwithstanding that a daughter is married to another family, the fact is that she is still her father's blood descendant whom the father recognizes. Therefore, it is reasonable and fair that a daughter should be given the right to inherit her father's property on the grounds of filial ties.

On the other hand, in Islam, a woman does not loose her identity and family lineal background as a result of her marriage. While a woman after her marriage takes on a new marital identity and may be called the wife of somebody, she still retains her old lineal one. Certain kinship rights and obligations of both husband and wife are not fundamentally affected by marriage. Moreover in view of the fact that the right of inheritance under Islamic law is also based on relationship of blood, a daughter is granted the right to inherit her deceased father's property on the grounds of blood relationship and to preserve filial ties.

The reason why the general rule of Igbo, Yoruba and Benin customary laws denies a wife the right to inherit her husband's property is that inheritance under these laws is limited to blood descendants. In view of the fact that a wife is not a blood descendant of her husband, she is not entitled to inherit any portion of his property notwithstanding her contributions towards the acquisition of the property.

The exception to this general rule in some Igbo communities where a widow has the right to inherit certain properties of her husband is commendable. The right should not be subject to the condition when a husband is not survived by any son. The communities should be more progressive and modify their laws to grant a widow the full right to inherit the property of her husband whether or not he is survived by a son.

Granted that a wife is not a blood descendant of her husband, disinheritance of a wife is unfair where the wife has contributed to the acquisition of the property. Though not all wives will fit into this category, it is only fair that a wife should be entitled to inherit some portion of her husband's property on the grounds of marital relationship or as a reward for marital devotion and domestic services. Besides, a wife is one of the persons who ordinarily will suffer as a result of the death of her husband.

In contrast with the customary laws, the rationale behind the Islamic law rule of inheritance which gives a wife the right to inherit the property of her husband is that one the law considers the wife to be among the primary dependants that the deceased maintained during his life-time. A wife should therefore be provided for from the property of her deceased husband so as to reduce her financial suffering as a result of her husband's death.

4.2 WOMEN'S INHERITANCE RIGHTS IN SOME AFRICAN COUNTRIES

A considerable hurdle to the realization of women's human rights in Africa is the pervasive denial of a woman's right to inherit land and other property. In many traditional societies in sub-Saharan Africa, land use, housing, and the transfer of land and housing between generations is regulated by customary law, which largely excludes women from property ownership and inheritance. Without secured land and property rights, widows and orphans are often left homeless and destitute after the death of their husband or father. Disinheritance seriously undermines women's economic security and independence as well as their access to adequate food and housing. The denial of land rights to women also contributes to the feminization of poverty and stunted economic development in countries where harmful inheritance practices are common.

An overview of inheritance laws and practices in Botswana, Zambia and Ghana is examined in this research work. Botswana, Zambia and Ghana have achieved varying degree of success in changing their inheritance law to a lesser degree. Ultimately, the inability of the laws to impact cultural practices has drastically limited their effectiveness.

As language recognizing and respecting women's rights inches its way into the constitutions and laws of many sub-Saharan African countries, there remains a considerable disconnect between official policy and actual practice. Many countries are characterized by a dual system of law that both espouse concepts of equal rights and at the same time legitimize traditional practices steeped in harmful acts of gender bias.

As will be illustrated by the following overview of inheritance laws and practices in Botswana, Zambia, and Ghana, official efforts to remedy discriminatory inheritance laws have typically taken place at the statutory level. These statutory changes generally have no practical effect on the great majority of the population, who are governed, in family and personal matters, by customary law. Short-sighted legislation attempting to change the customary law, while facially progressive, is practically stillborn. Legislators have seemingly ignored the cultural realities of their countries and have passed laws that are largely unpopular and consequently ineffective. To develop systems of inheritance that truly respect women's rights, laws must be written and implemented in ways that recognize and respect the cultural traditions in which these systems are based. Laws that ignore this reality are doomed to be ineffective and ultimately irrelevant.

Land and housing in most traditional african cultures is regulated by customary law. Although varying to a certain degree from culture to culture, women are generally prohibited by customary law from owning or inheriting land or other property. Land ownership traditionally is passed through male heirs. A woman's right to access and use land has customarily been defined solely by her relation to men.

While married, a woman enjoys the use of land belonging to her husband; while single, she has access to that of her father or guardian.

When a husband or father dies, a woman's right to the land is suddenly placed in jeopardy.

In most ethnic groups, such as the Ewe in Ghana, customary systems traditionally included a social safety net providing for widows and orphans at the death of the male head of household. While women were not able to directly inherit land or property, the men that did inherit were required to care for the wife or wives of the decedent and all of his dependents as the decedent would have. The heir thus not only inherited the property, but he also "inherited" the responsibility to provide for all who depended on the property for their livelihood.[65]

4.2.1 COUNTRY OVERVIEWS

---

[65] Richardson, Abby Morrow. "Women's Inheritance Rights in Africa: The Need to Integrate Cultural Understanding and Legal Reform." Human Rights Brief 11, no. 2 (2004): 19-22.

BOTSWANA, ZAMBIA, AND GHANA have achieved varying degrees of success in changing their inheritance laws and, to a lesser degree, their inheritance practices. Ultimately, the inability of the laws to impact cultural practice has drastically limited their effectiveness.

D) BOTSWANA

The Botswana legal system is derived from five primary sources: the Botswana Constitution, Roman Dutch Law, statutory law passed by the parliament, case law, and customary law. Botswana is also party to regional and international treaties requiring statutory compliance with their anti-discrimination standards, including the UN Convention on the Elimination of All Forms of Discrimination Against Women (CEDAW) and the Southern Africa Development Community (SADC) Declaration on Gender and Development, promoting the prevention and eradication of violence against women and children in sub-Saharan Africa. Efforts to bring national laws in conformity with these international obligations have been piecemeal and largely insignificant.

The Constitution, common law, and statutory law all contain provisions prohibiting discrimination generally, although discrimination against women is sometimes excepted. For example, section 15 of the Bill of Rights prohibits the making of any law that is "discriminatory either of itself or in its effect," defining discrimination as affording different treatment to people based on "race, tribe, place of origin, political opinions, colour or creed." Discrimination on the basis of sex is notably absent from this definition, although in one significant case, *Unity Dow v. Attorney General*, Botswana's high court interpreted the provision to include sex discrimination. Section 15 also contains certain express exemptions: laws and practices pertaining to adoption, marriage, burial, devolution of property upon death and other matters related to personal law do not have to comport with the non-discrimination provision. These exemptions encompass practices that most affect the lives and rights of Batswana women, and especially their right to inherit.

Statutory law contains similar provisions depriving women of inheritance rights. The Administration of Estates Act states that every person belonging to an ethnic group, which essentially applies to every native citizen of Botswana, will have their property devolved according to the customs and practices of their particular ethnic group. Unless one affirmatively signs a form excluding customary law from his or her life, a drastic measure which most would not consider, custom will dictate how property is divided. If one foregoes all customary law, there is a statutory scheme of inheritance based on community property, written wills, and intestate succession laws, similar to those found in most western countries, that provides for the inheritance of widows and children. For the great majority of the Batswana people, however, there is no codified law of succession.

For the great majority of the Botswana people, however, there is no codified law of succession.

Throughout Botswana, women are excluded from the great majority of traditional leadership positions. Within a family, the father is the customary head. According to the patrilineal system of marriage that most Botswana follow, a married woman belongs to her husband's ethnic group. Most of the property owned or acquired by the couple in the course of the marriage belongs to the husband and will pass to the eldest son at his father's death. A woman retains, in theory, the right to certain property, such as her plowing fields, which are intended to pass to her daughter upon her death. The male household head, however, determines whether the property will go with the daughter into her marriage. Although this land and all decisions regarding it should technically belong to the woman, the male household head has the power to make all determinations about land transfer in his family. He can divest the woman of her access to the land at will.

In Botswana and many other southern and West African countries, disinherited women have an aversion to the formal court system.

Although a woman may take her relatives to court to challenge the way in which they divided her husband's property, this action would be seen as a declaration of war against the husband's family, resulting in a traumatic severance of the widow's and her children's family ties. Widows face other institutional disincentives to court action. Courts are often located in central hubs that are difficult for poor rural women to reach. Judges are sometimes perceived as biased, unfair, and responsive to bribery and coercion by the other party. The woman is often ostracized or ridiculed by the community and threatened or harassed by the in-laws. Finally, the decisions made at the court level, if they favor the woman, are often not enforced.

Customary law and practices vary from tribe to tribe, and also within tribes, but are largely based on similar social principles. Throughout Botswana, women are excluded from the great majority of traditional leadership positions. Within a family, the father is the customary head. According to the patrilineal system of marriage that most Botswana follow, a married woman belongs to her husband's ethnic group. Most of the property owned or acquired by the couple in the course of the marriage belongs to the husband and will pass to the eldest son at his father's death. A woman retains, in theory, the right to certain property, such as her plowing fields, which are intended to pass to her daughter upon her death. The male household head, however, determines whether the property will go with the daughter into her marriage. Although this land and all decisions regarding it should technically belong to the woman, the male household head has the power to make all determinations about land transfer in his family. He can divest the woman of her access to the land at will.

Widows face other institutional disincentives to court action. Courts are often located in central hubs that are difficult for poor rural women to reach. Judges are sometimes perceived as biased, unfair, and responsive to bribery and coercion by the other party. The woman is often ostracized or ridiculed by the community and threatened or harassed by the in-laws. Finally, the decisions made at the court level, if they favor the woman, are often not enforced.[66]

---

[66] http://digitalcommons.wcl.american.edu/hrbrief/vol11/iss2/6 OP.cit Richardson, Abby Morrow. "Women's Inheritance Rights in Africa: The Need to Integrate Cultural Understanding and Legal Reform."

E) ZAMBIA

Zambia, like Botswana, has a dual legal system: statutory, constitutional, and common law coexist with a parallel yet sometimes contradictory customary law system. The Zambian Constitution also has a Bill of Rights that guarantees equal protection under the law to all citizens. Zambia has ratified CEDAW and other international human rights treaties, but it has not incorporated them into its domestic legal system. Like Botswana, the Zambian Constitution excludes from its equal protection and anti-discrimination provisions practices pertaining to marriage, divorce, devolution of property, and other personal and family matters. In these areas of critical concern for women, the law legitimizes a discriminatory customary system.

In 1989, Zambia enacted the Intestate Succession Act (Act), which significantly affected a woman's legal rights to inherit. The Act, which governs the administration of an estate when there is no will, establishes the spouse (male or female) as the primary inheritor of the descendant's estate. It guarantees a life interest in the marital home for the surviving spouse. Although beneficial to women because it secures their right to remain in their home, the law falls short of granting equal inheritance rights to women. The widow does not inherit the title to the home; instead, she may only stay until her own death or remarriage. She gains only the usufruct right of use, not absolute ownership.

Human Rights Brief 11, no. 2 (2004): 19-22.

Additionally, enforcement of the Intestate Succession Act requires a widow to take her case before a statutory court, which, for the reasons mentioned above for Batswana women, is not a realistic option for most Zambian women.

Customary law in Zambia varies among the country's seventy-three ethnic groups. Of these groups, sixty-nine are matrilineal, meaning that lineages and families are traced to a female ancestor, and the blood line is traced through the female members of the family.

Despite the centrality of matrilineal women to the definition of family and ancestry, men in matrilineal societies, like their patrilineal counterparts, wield the actual power. Men are the traditional leaders who sit as chiefs and headmen and preside over traditional courts.

Customary law relating to inheritance in matrilineal societies provides that when a man dies, his primary heirs are his nephews (his sisters' children). This matrilineal system of inheritance stands in direct contrast to the Intestate Succession Act, which devises an inheritance scheme that is patrilineal. The Act establishes certain inheritance rights for the spouse, dependents, and the decedent's parents.

The direct conflict of this Act with the practice of land distribution among the large majority of Zambian families has severely limited its applicability and effectiveness.

In Zambia, as in Botswana, the dual system of law simultaneously promotes concepts of equality and anti-discrimination and allows a discriminatory system of customary law to govern the majority of matters affecting an ordinary citizen's life. Although the provisions of the Intestate Succession Act are available to all

Zambians, it is largely ignored and disfavored by local courts since its terms are foreign to the family systems in which the majority of Zambians live. As human rights organizations seek to change cultural understandings about women's inheritance rights, the statutory law should also be sensitive to the context in which it will be applied. It should not seek to usurp the entire familial system on which much of Zambian society is based, but it should rather create ways to protect women's rights that are more familiar, less threatening, and that can be better integrated into traditional cultural structures.[67]

F) GHANA

Ghana is widely seen as a leader in the struggle for inheritance rights in Africa. In addition to having ratified numerous international human rights treaties, including CEDAW and the African Charter on Human and Peoples' Rights, Ghana passed, in 1985, the Intestate Succession Law (the Provisional National Defense Council, or PNDC Law 111 significantly altered the system of land and property distribution legally recognized by the Ghanaian government. According to its accompanying memorandum, the law seeks to "provide a uniform intestate succession law that will be applicable throughout the country irrespective of the class of the intestate and the type of marriage [statutory or customary] contracted by him or her."

---

[67] Published by Digital Commons @ American University Washington College of Law, 2004 Op.cit Richardson, Abby Morrow. "Women's Inheritance Rights in Africa: The Need to Integrate Cultural Understanding and Legal Reform." Human Rights Brief 11, no. 2 (2004): 19-22..
PNDC, Law 111).

The law, "aimed at giving a larger portion of the estate of the deceased to his spouse than is normally the case at present," grants concrete rights to spouses to the property acquired by the decedent during his or her lifetime. This notably does not include family and lineage property. Despite this omission, the Act states that wives and children may remain in the home as tenants in common until the widow's death or remarriage.

PNDC Law 111 was enshrined in the 1992 Constitution with clauses addressing the property rights of spouses. The Constitution states in article 22 that "spouses shall have equal access to property jointly acquired during marriage" and that "a spouse shall not be deprived of a reasonable provision out of the estate of a spouse whether or not the spouse died having made a will." With these provisions explicitly providing for women's inheritance, Ghanaian constitutional law goes well beyond that of Botswana and Zambia in legally preserving women's rights. No exceptions exist for the application of customary law in Ghana.

Customary law, however, persists despite these laws. Ghana contains both matrilineal (in the Upper East, Upper West, and South western regions) and patrilineal (in the Northern, Volta, Greater Accra, and Southern regions) ethnic groups. In addition, nearly half of all marriages in Ghana are officially polygamous, while a much greater number consist of a husband with one official wife and one or more concubines.

Under customary law, when a man dies, all of his self-acquired property (which often includes property acquired with the assistance and labour of his wife) returns to his lineage and is distributed accordingly.

In patrilineal societies, as in most of Botswana, the land will thus go to a son or brother. In matrilineal societies, as in most of Zambia, the property will devolve to nephews. In both systems, the widow is usually entirely dispossessed.

With the advent of PNDC Law 111, entire systems of property inheritance and distribution were legally uprooted, particularly those in matrilineal lineages. The legal revolution, however, has not fully translated into cultural transformation. In many ways, the law is impractical in matrilineal communities whose entire social and familial system would be completely debased if the law were to be implemented.

The law also fails to mention or recognize polygamous marriages, which constitute the majority of marriages in Ghana. When applied to these unions, the law fails to adequately address the multitude of complexities arising when a man dies leaving multiple wives and multiple sets of children.

An even greater obstacle to the law's implementation is the lack of public education about the law. Today, 19 years after PNDC Law 111 was passed, many people who do not belong to the educated, urban classes are not aware of the law's existence. There is no public education program designed to inform the Ghanaian citizenry of this significant aspect of their legal system. Customary inheritance systems persist and customary courts continue to resolve conflicts.

The Ghanaian inheritance situation in many ways is a step beyond Botswana and Zambia. Nonetheless, the full implementation of women's inheritance rights is still far from complete.

Ghanaians should be informed about the law and know how to access it. Future laws should not ignore the reality of the cultural situation in which they are to be applied; otherwise, they will risk being ignored and ineffective.[68]

4.3 SPECIFIC OBSTACLES TO WOMEN'S INHERITANCE RIGHTS

a) Legal Obstacles

Inadequate laws regulating administration of deceased estate particularly at federal level constitutes a major obstacle to women's inheritance rights.

Compounding this problem is also our legal system which gives rise to the operation of at least a tripartite system of laws that function simultaneously. The existing laws dealing with inheritance and succession are not entirely free from sexist biases.[69]

Furthermore, there is gap between law and practice. For example, on intestacy customary law applies notwithstanding the fact that the parties have entered into statutory marriage.

b) Political Obstacles

---

[68] Richardson, Abby Morrow. "Women's Inheritance Rights in Africa: The Need to Integrate Cultural Understanding and Legal Reform." Human Rights Brief 11, no. 2 (2004): 19-22.
[69] A reading of section 120(b) of the Administration and Succession (Estate of Deceased Persons) Law illustrates the gender biases in our laws.

Generally speaking, Nigerian women are politically marginalized. They lack access to power and decision-making positions through which meaningful changes can be realised.

Government political appointments hardly favour women. They have always been tokens. For meaningful progress, women's political participation must be full and not mere tokenism.

c) Socio-Cultural Obstacles

Women's social status is still very low. This is mainly due to illiteracy, poverty and cultural practices, which treat women as mini persons, objects of inheritance rather than subjects of inheritance. The traditional, cultural and religious beliefs that women are inferior and subordinate to men tend to perpetuate widespread practices involving violence and very harmful to women. The discrimination in education of girls and boys is borne out of this patriarchal attitude including son preference ideology. Frequent importation of native law and custom of inheritance to execution of wills of a testator duly made under the Wills Act results in hardship to even wives of statutory law marriage. For example, if a testator bequeaths his matrimonial home to his wife in perpetuity, objections are raised to the execution of that bequest on the ground that by native law and custom of Igbos, for example, a man's dwelling house (matrimonial home) belongs to his eldest son or to his male next of- kin where he is not survived by any male issue.

d) Economic Obstacles

Women's economic status has further jeopardized their inheritance rights. Women, owing to several factors, lack access to means of production and since a woman's right to property is subject to varying traditional and cultural practices, her ability to secure credit is undermined.

Women in Nigeria perform multiple economic and household responsibilities in the face of systematic discrimination in accessing the basic technologies and resources which are required in order to function in an economically productive and efficient manner. This discrimination imposes considerable limits on women's capacity to participate in development. The role of women in Nigerian economy is largely unrecognised.

e) **Religion as an Obstacle**

Both religions practised in Nigeria – Christianity and Islam - militate against women's rights to inheritance. A woman is not viewed as man's equal, consequently both religions will hardly concede equality of share in inheritance. The varying systems of religion relegate woman to the background thereby reinforcing the inferiority of women.

5.0.0 CONCLUSION

Under the hybrid legal system which operates in Nigeria, the received English laws, local statutes, customary laws of various tribes and Islamic law govern inheritance. The received English laws on inheritance on testate and intestate succession and the administration of Estates laws of States which have such laws do not deprive women of the rights of inheritance to the estate of their husbands or their fathers. Regrettably, many women who contracted marriage under the Marriage Act and who should benefit from these laws are not aware of the laws.

There has not been any concerted action by women's movement towards enhancing inheritance rights of women in Nigeria. Their work has been disjunctive and as such, no desired national impact has been made. The reason for this may be partly because the status of women in Nigeria with respect to inheritance is not the same everywhere. Some women, particularly women married under the Act (statutory marriage), enjoy better inheritance rights and may not be bothered about the situation of other women subject to customary laws.

The work of NGOs concerned with the promotion of women's rights in Nigeria has been mainly at the level of advocacy – creating awareness about the type of marriage that will give a woman better inheritance rights and encouraging men to make wills. This lop-sided type of advocacy that is not targeted at influencing laws and policies pertaining to inheritance rights have not improved in any way the status of women in Nigeria vis-à-vis inheritance rights.

The Nigerian government has not done well either.

There is a clear lack of political will to effect any legislative changes particularly at Federal (National) level. All the recommendations of the Law Reform Commission relating to family and personal laws are yet to be promulgated into law that will ensure that all marriages recognised under the law enjoy equal status.

Furthermore, there is lack of economic and political will to use existing governmental structures – for example, Federal and State Ministries of Women Affairs and Social Justice and

National Commission on Human Rights - to improve women's rights to inheritance.

Although the Constitution of the Federal Republic of Nigeria 1999, in section 42, prohibits discrimination on grounds of sex, item 62 of the Exclusive Legislative List precludes the federal government from legislating on the formation, annulment and dissolution of marriages contracted under Islamic and customary law, including matrimonial causes thereto. This leaves important issues that have enormous implications for women in Nigeria to various States that make up the federation to individually decide.

The Nigerian government has ratified the Convention on Elimination of All forms of Discrimination Against Women (CEDAW: 1979) without any reservation and also the African

Charter on Human and Peoples Rights (1981),[70] which requires states to eliminate all forms of discrimination against women recognised in International Conventions and Declarations.[71] Consequently, it is expected that the government should adopt appropriate legislation and actions aimed at modifying discriminatory laws, regulations, customs and practices against

women.[72]

As at now, there is no national committee charged with the supervision of implementation of CEDAW in Nigeria.

5.1.0 FINDINGS

Based on our findings, there are certain obstacles to woman's inheritance rights in Nigeria which are as follows:

5.1.1 Our findings on the received English law on inheritance on testacy, that is, the

Will Act of 1837 do not ordinarily deprive women of the right of inheritance. However, a man in exercising his unlimited freedom to dispose of his estate as he wishes in a Will could deprive his wife or daughter of the right to inherit his property if he fails to make provisions for either of them in his Will. There is nothing the wife or daughter can do if the Will complies with the formalities prescribed by the Wills Act of 1837 for making a valid Will.

---

[70] The Charter is now part of our domestic law by virtue of its incorporation –CAP 10 Laws of the Federation of Nigeria, 1990.
[71] Article 18(3) of the Charter
[72] Articles 2(f) and 16 of CEDAW.

The English Wills Act of 1837 has since been abrogated in England. New laws have since been enacted to restrain the testamentary freedom of a testator such that wife, children and other dependants of a testator who have been deprived of the right to inherit his estates in a Will could be given a reasonable financial provision from the net estate by a court of competent jurisdiction on application by such persons.[73] The provisions of the new laws can be said to have somehow conferred on a wife or a daughter who has been deprived of the right to inherit the estates of her husband or her father in a Will, a limited right of inheritance of such estate.

It is regrettable that despite the fact that the Wills Act of 1837 is no longer operative in England, the Act is still applicable in many States of Nigeria except in few States which have enacted their own Will Laws.[74]

It is gratifying however that the States that have enacted Wills laws have followed the modern trend in England and some other developed countries to restrain the testamentary freedom of a testator under their Wills Laws. Hence, there is need for other States in Nigeria that have not enacted statutes on Wills to take a cue from those States.

---

[73] Inheritance (Family Provision) Act 1938 as amended by the Intestate Estates Act 1952 and Inheritance (Provision for Family and Dependants Act 1975).

[74] Wills Law of Lagos State *CAPW2 Laws of Lagos State of Nigeria 2003*; Wills Edict of Oyo State *CAP 63 Laws of Oyo State of Nigeria 1990.* Kaduna State Wills Edict. *CAP 163 Laws of Kaduna State of Nigeria 1991.* Kwara State Wills Edict. *CAP 168 Laws of Kwara State of Nigeria 1994,* Anambra State Administration and Succession (Estate of Deceased Persons) Law. *CAP4. Laws of Anambra State of Nigeria 1987.*

5.1.2. Our findings in respect of Igbo, Benin and Yoruba customary laws of inheritance reveal that there are local variations to the general rule of inheritance of the customary laws of these ethnic groups that women as wives and daughters are not entitled to inherit the property of their deceased husbands and fathers. In some Igbo communities of Arochuckwu, a wife inherits her husband's economic plants and trees. In Ekiti Division, a wife inherits such property if the husband is not survived by any son. In Mbaino, a wife inherits such property subject to overall control of herself and the property by the eldest nearest paternal relation of her husband.[75]

The local variations as regards the customary law that daughters do not have the right to inherit the property of their fathers are found in Ohafia Division where a man's compound is inherited by his sons and daughters as a body. In the same Division, where a man is survived by only daughters, the daughters inherit his compound or any of his other lands and houses with the eldest full brother of the deceased in control. In Oraukwu town in Idemile Division, a daughter on whom the *nrachi* ceremony has been performed inherits her father's compound, other lands and houses.[76]

The variation under the Benin customary law of inheritance is that where the eldest surviving child of a deceased Benin man is a female, she could be given a reasonable share of the deceased property with mutual agreement of the family elders and other children.[77]

---

[75] *Customary Law Manual* op cit at page 113.
[76] Ibid. page 103.
[77] *Handbook on Benin Customs and Usages* op cit at page 13.

Notwithstanding the variations of the customary laws of inheritance of Igbo and Benin where wives and daughters are given limited rights to inherit the estates of their husbands and fathers, these are just few exceptions to the general rule which disinherits many women. Moreover, the reasonable share of the estate which Benin custom allows a daughter who is the eldest surviving child of a Benin man to be given from his father's property is not of right but it is dependent on the whims and caprices of the other children and elders of the family.

In this connection, the Benin and Igbo customary laws of inheritance which deprive women as wives and daughters, of the right to inherit the property of their husbands and fathers because they are females are discriminatory against women. In the same vein, the Yoruba customary law which deprives wives of the right to inherit the estates of their husbands is also discriminatory.

These customary laws are not only unjust but also unconstitutional as they violate the provisions of Section 42 (1) of the 1999 Constitution of the Federal Republic of Nigeria which forbids discrimination by reason of sex. Section 42(1) of the Constitution provides:[78]

> A citizen of Nigeria of a particular community, ethnic group, place of origin, sex, religion or political opinion shall not, by reason only that he is such a person –

---

[78] *CAP C 23 Laws of Federation of Nigeria 2004*

(a) Be subjected either expressly by, or in the practical application of any law in force in Nigeria or any executive or administrative action of the government, to disabilities or restrictions to which citizens of Nigeria of other communities, ethnic groups, places of origin, sex, religions or political opinions are not made subject.

The import of this provision is to protect the rights of all citizens of Nigeria, male or female against any form of discrimination by reason of sex, religion, ethnicity etc. which may be imposed by any law operating in Nigeria. Therefore, there is need to reform these customary laws so that women can have the rights to inherit the property of their deceased husbands and fathers.

5.1.3 On the other hand, Islamic law which regulates the lives of muslims accord women, as wives and daughters the rights of inheritance of the property of their deceased husbands and fathers. Specific shares of the deceased estates are allocated to them in the Holy Quran. The Holy Quran being a divine book revealed by Allah is sacred and immutable. Therefore, the rights of women as wives and daughters to inheritance under Islamic law are indefeasible. In this connection, Islamic law of inheritance, unlike the customary laws of inheritance of Igbo, Benin and Yoruba people not only accord women as wives and daughters the rights of inheritance but better rights of inheritance.

However, in States of Southern Nigeria where Islamic law has not been officially established, it seems probable that many matters of inheritance and succession affecting

Muslims which should have been dealt with under Islamic law are still being dealt with under customary law by customary law courts legally established in the States.

It is noteworthy to say that the fervent desire of Muslims in Lagos State to have Islamic personal law matters affecting Muslims determined according to Islamic law has led to the establishment of an Independent Shariah Panel under the auspices of Lagos State Chapter of the Supreme Council for Shariah in Nigeria to adjudicate on Islamic personal law matters in accordance with Islamic law as they affect Muslims who have voluntarily submitted themselves to the judgment of the panel.[79]

Although, the panel was not established by legal or constitutional instrument, the panel has satisfactorily adjudicated on Islamic personal law matters as regards marriage, divorce, custody etc. The efforts of the panel are therefore commendable because the panel has lived up to the yearnings of pious Muslims in the State for matters affecting them to be determined in accordance with Islamic law.

Professor Auwalu .H. Yadudu who wrote the preface to the selected judgments of the panel stated thus:

> The analysis of laws, consideration of social and political matters and the review of fact contained in

---

[79] The Selected Judgment of the Lagos State Independent Shariah Panel Vol. I (Published by graphix solutions suite Nigeria 2005).

these decisions and the personnel who have rendered them have, without doubt, portrayed a breadth and depth of knowledge of Shariah principles, Nigerian law and procedure that can rival decisions of the higher bench in the Nigerian Court System: both the Shariah, and common law types.[80]

5.1.4 Our findings also reveal that Imo and Enugu States which are predominantly Igbo people have recently enacted laws which have given women the right to inherit the estates of their deceased husbands and fathers. These laws seem to have abolished the Igbo customary law of inheritance that deprives women, as daughters and wives of the rights of inheritance. In fact, section 4 (c) of Imo State law on Elimination of all Forms of Gender Based Discrimination and Inequalities[81] specifically states thus: 'any existing laws, regulations, customs and practices, which constitute discrimination against any person, shall be null and void and of no effect whatsoever and shall not be enforceable against any person'.

While these laws are progressive, many people are not aware of them. It would appear that women are yet to benefit from these laws. Therefore, there is need for the governments of those States to publicize the laws.

5.2.0 RECOMMENDATIONS

---

[80] Ibid.
[81] Law No. 7 Imo State of Nigeria 2007.

Based on our findings, the following recommendations are made:

5.2.1 LAW REFORM

Harmonisation of received English law, local statutes and customary laws, particularly in the area of family law – marriage and inheritance is very important. This has been done in Tanzania successfully. In fact, it was one of the first countries in Africa to attempt the unification of customary laws in its various tribes.

Kenya has made several attempts to solve the problem of multiplicity of personal laws but like Nigeria, it has not been successful. Although it is recognised that law is not a panacea for 22 all problems, it is a very useful beginning that can ensure that the different types of marriages enjoy social and legal parity of status.

5.2.2 Institutional Reform

Institutional reform to support legislative reforms is important. For example, specific legal aid for women; appeal office for discriminatory practices; gender specific data collection and dissemination facilities.

5.2.3. Mass Enlightenment Campaign

Mass campaign should be mounted by the Ministry of Women Affairs at both the

Federal and State levels to enlighten people first about the hardship and injustice which the discriminatory customary laws impose on women. Secondly, to make people appreciate that the basis for which custom denied women the right to inherit property in the past is no longer sustainable in contemporary times. Therefore, there is need to reform the laws. The campaign should be through jingles on electronic media, discussions over the radio, advertisements on bill boards, in newspapers in both English and local languages so as to reach the literate and illiterate members of the public. These enlightenment programmes are necessary to change the social attitudes of the people particularly the men.

A change of the social attitudes of the men will, after sometime, make men to respect the personality of women, change the popular misconception that women are inferior to men and eventually facilitate a reform of the customary laws.

5.2.4 States' Laws on Inheritance

The reform of these customary laws on inheritance starting from the grassroots should be followed by legislation. Such legislation should abolish the indigenous customary laws of inheritance and thus give women the rights to inherit the property of their deceased husbands and fathers. The laws should specify the shares which wives and daughters are entitled to inherit. Such laws should be applicable and enforceable in the respective States. If this is done, the other States of the Federation will be emulating Imo, Enugu and Cross River States that have enacted such laws.[82] However, the proposed new States' laws on inheritance should operate without prejudice to Islamic law of inheritance which gives women better rights of inheritance.

---

[82] Gender and Equal Opportunities Law No 7 of Imo State 2007; The Prohibition of Infringement of a Widow's and Widower's Fundamental Rights Law of Enugu State 2001; Cross River Female Person's Inheritance of Property law 2007

It is pertinent to state that Section 4 (2) of the Enugu State Law on inheritance which provides that a Widow/ Widower shall not be dispossessed on the death of the husband/wife of property acquired in the deceased husband's/wife's lifetime without his/her consent is ambiguous. To that extent it is defective. Therefore, there is need for the State legislature to take urgent action to amend the law to specifically provide for the rights of inheritance for daughters and wives in the property of their deceased fathers and husbands.

5.2.5 Enlightenment Programmes for Women

Be that as it may, it is pertinent to emphasize that legislation to eliminate discrimination against women's rights of inheritance is not enough. Educational and enlightenment programmes are also necessary to inform women themselves about the inheritance law. This is because many women, owing to illiteracy or ignorance are not aware of the existing laws on inheritance which provide the rights of inheritance for them. Even the educated ones who have some knowledge of the laws do not bother to know the contents of such laws and how they can access the laws to protect their rights of inheritance.

In this connection, women social groups/organisations, religious leaders in rural communities, non-governmental organisations, mass media, Ministries of Women Affairs and Justice at both Federal and State levels should embark on educational and enlightenment programmes to educate women of their rights of inheritance under the existing laws. It is hoped that such concerted efforts will help to promote women's rights of inheritance.

5.2.6 Role of the Judiciary

Our courts should be bold and imaginative in their determination of issues on customary laws affecting inheritance rights of women. Any customary law that precludes women from inheriting the property of their husbands and parents should be declared invalid on the grounds that it is unconstitutional and repugnant to natural justice, equity and good conscience. In this way, the judiciary will help to develop our customary laws to meet changes in global trends to women's rights and uphold the fundamental human rights of women as guaranteed under our Constitution.

5.2.7 Enactment of New Wills Laws

States that have not enacted Wills Laws should enact such laws to replace the English Wills Acts of 1837 and 1852 that are still applicable in those states. The new Will Laws of the States should emulate the Wills Laws of Lagos, Oyo, Kaduna and Kwara States.[83] These laws have curbed the testamentary freedom of a testator by making provision for courts to make financial provisions for spouses, children and other dependants of a testator who has failed to provide for such persons in his Will.

---

[83] Section 2 Wills Law of Lagos State. *CAP 2 Laws of Lagos State 2003*; S.4 Wills Edict Oyo State *CAP 63 Laws of Oyo State of Nigeria 1990*; S.5 Kaduna State Wills Edict *CAP 163 Laws of Kaduna State of Nigeria 1991*; S.5 Kwara State Wills Edict *CAP 168 Laws of Kwara State of Nigeria 1994;*

5.2.8 Free Legal Aid for Matters Relating to the Rights of Inheritance

Free legal aid services should be provided by the Legal Aid Council for poor women to seek redress in courts in cases of the violation of their rights of inheritance. It is pertinent to state that the Legal Aid Council Act[84] presently empowers the Legal Aid Council to render free legal assistance in respect of civil claims to cover breach of fundamental human rights as guaranteed under Chapter IV of the Constitution. However, we suggest that the Federal Ministry of Women Affairs should initiate a bill to the National Assembly to amend the Legal Aid Council Act to specifically provide for civil matters relating to violation of women's right of inheritance. In the alternative, Nigeria should emulate some African Countries like Uganda and South Africa. These countries have enlarged the fundamental rights provisions in their Constitutions to give any person, organisation or association the right to apply to courts for the enforcement of the rights of the underprivileged, the poor or literates whose fundamental human rights are being violated or have been violated.[85]

The proposed amendment to the Constitution should give individuals and non-governmental organisations the right to institute legal action against any persons or organisations who violate inheritance rights of women. This will make women to have better

---

[84] CAP L 9. Laws of the Federation of Nigeria 2004.
[85] Section 32 Constitution of the Republic of Uganda 1995, Section 38 Constitution of the Republic of South Africa 1996.

access to legal representation when their rights of inheritance are violated or about to be violated.

It is important to mention that section 15 (2) of Ugandan Constitution specifically prohibits laws, cultures, customs and traditions which are against the dignity or interests of women. Our National Assembly should amend our Constitution to include such a provision. This will ensure the abolition of all customary laws that are discriminatory against women as regards the right of inheritance.

5.2.9 States' Laws on Administration of Estates

States that have not enacted Administration of Estates laws should enact such laws to replace the received English laws applicable to the estates of an intestate in Nigeria. The new laws should be made to cover the estates of intestates who contract monogamous and polygamous marriages. This will be in line with the provision of Intestate Succession Act of Zambia.[86] Section 3 of the Zambian law on Interpretation defines marriage to include a polygamous marriage. In this regard, the Zambian law is progressive and needs to be emulated by Nigeria and other African Countries which are interested in promoting the rights of women.

5.2.1.0 Establishment of Shariah Courts in the States of Southern Nigeria

The governments of the States in Southern Nigeria where Muslims are predominant should enact laws to establish Shariah courts of co-ordinate jurisdiction with customary courts existing presently in

---

[86] Intestate Succession Act No. 5 of Zambia 1989

those States with jurisdiction over Islamic personal law on matrimonial and succession matters as provided by the Constitution. Alternatively, the governments of the States where Muslims are not many could create a department of Shariah within the existing customary courts system to deal with Islamic personal law matters.

Persons with basic qualifications for appointment as Qadis (Islamic Judges) should be appointed for Shariah Courts of subordinate jurisdictions with customary courts. As regards the department of Shariah, persons knowledgeable about Islamic Law should be appointed as judicial personnel to manage the department. The jurisdiction of Shariah courts of subordinate jurisdiction with customary courts or the responsibility of the Shariah department should include services as regards the distribution of the estates of Muslims according to Islamic law. The distribution of the estates of the Muslims according to Islamic law of inheritance will no doubt enable Muslim women in those States to enjoy the right of inheritance accorded them under Islamic law.

5.2.1.1 ECONOMIC EMPOWERMENT OF WOMEN

Besides legal approach this study recommends that women should be empowered economically so that they can have resources that will make them less dependent on men. In view of the fact that majority of women in both urban and rural areas engage in small businesses, petty trading and processing of agricultural produce, they should be educated and encouraged by women's associations and non-government agencies working for women to organise themselves into small cooperative groups.

Such cooperatives groups should be assisted with soft loans by local and state governments as part of their poverty alleviation programmes. The soft loans can help the businesses of the women to grow gradually and thereby increase their resources over the years. The poverty alleviation programmes of governments should also include skill acquisition training for women in urban and rural areas that will make women self-reliant economically.

In addition, while alive, men should endeavour to set up small businesses for their wives to enable them have resources of their own. Women should be allowed and encouraged by their husbands to control their resources for effective economic empowerment. The control of their financial resources by women over the years will enable them not only to fight for their rights of inheritance under the laws but also make them less dependent on inheritance from their deceased husbands and fathers. They will then be able to take care of themselves and their children on the demise of their relations.

BIBLIOGRAPHY

(1956), SCNLR 265, <u>Gbadamosi Rafiu V Silifatu Abasi</u>(1996) 7 SCNJ 53 at page 55.

(1962) 1 ALL NLR 702; <u>Adeniyi V Adeniyi</u> (1972) I ALL NLR 301.

(1963) 1 All N.L.R 352.

 (1963) 1 ALL N.L.R 352.

(1972) 10 SC 126.

(1989) 2 NWLR (pt 104)373.

(19890 2 NWLR (pt 104)373

 (1997) 7 NWLR (Pt 512) 283.

(2000) 5 NWLR (pt 657) 402.

(2001) 11 NWLR (pt 723)196.

(PNDC, Law 111).

A reading of section 120(b) of the Administration and Succession (Estate of Deceased Persons) Law illustrates the gender biases in our laws.

Adesunbokan v. *Yunusa* [1968] N.N.L.R. 79.

Ahmadu Sidi v. Abdulahi Sha'aban [1992] 4 NWLR p. 113.

Article 18(3) of the Charter

Articles 2(f) and 16 of CEDAW.

Bryson Valerie Op Cit page 16.

CAP C 23 Laws of Federation of Nigeria 2004

CAP L 9. Laws of the Federation of Nigeria 2004.

Chubb,Ibo land Tenure, zaria,1943,para 41.

Cited by Bryson Valerie in Feminist Debates Issues of theory and political practices (palgrate New York 1999) page 5.

Customary Law Manual op cit at page 113.

Customary law manual Op cit. pages 112-113. Arochukwu is in Abia state. Etiti is in Enugu and Mbano is in Imo State.

Customary Law Manual. The communities are in Aguata, Idemili; Ihiala, Ogbaru which are Local Government Areas of Anambra State; Mbaitoli, Ikeduru, Orlu, Mbano, Oguta, Okigwe are in Imo State; Igbo Eze, Nsukka, Ezeogu are in Enugu State.

E.I Nwogugu, family law in Nigeria (1974) Heinemann Studies in Nigeria law p.406.

E.I Nwogugu,Ibid at p.407; Mojekwu V Mojekwu(supra);Udensi V Mogbo (1976) 7 S.C.I.

E.I. Nwogugu,family law in Nigeria (1974) Heinemann Studies in Nigerian Law p.402.

Emiola A., *The Principles of African Customary Law* (Emiola Publishers, Ogbomoso, Nigeria, 1997) p. 122.

Freeman Marsha A: Women Development and Justice. Using the international Convention on Women's rights in Kerr(ed) ours by Right: Women's rights as Human Rights Op cit page 93.

Gender and equal opportunities law 2007 No 7 Imo state of Nigeria.

Gender and Equal Opportunities Law No 7 of Imo State 2007; The Prohibition of Infringement of a Widow's and Widower's Fundamental Rights Law of Enugu State 2001; Cross River Female Person's Inheritance of Property law 2007

Handbook on Benin Customs and Usages op cit at page 13.

Handbook on some Benin customs and usage.

http://digitalcommons.wcl.american.edu/hrbrief/vol11/iss2/6 OP.cit
Richardson, Abby Morrow. "Women's Inheritance Rights in Africa: The Need to Integrate Cultural Understanding and Legal Reform."

Human Rights Brief 11, no. 2 (2004): 19-22.

Inheritance (Family Provision) Act 1938 as amended by the Intestate Estates Act 1952 and Inheritance (Provision for Family and Dependants Act 1975).

Intestate Succession Act No. 5 of Zambia 1989

Joy Ezeilo, *Genderizing the Judiciary in Commonwealth Africa*" a paper presented at an International Conference on Gendering the Millennium, 11 – 13 September, 1998, University of Dundee, U.K..

Kasumu and Salacuse, *Nigerian Family Law*, (London: Butterworths, 1966), p. 262; (2) Obi, S.N.C., *Modern Family Law in Southern Nigeria*, (London: Sweet and Maxwell, 1966) p. 342 (3) Nwogugu E.I., *Family Law in Nigeria* op. cit., p.390.

Kerr Joanna (ed) Ours by Rights: Women Rights as Human Rights (Zed Books London 1993) page 93.

Law No. 7 Imo State of Nigeria 2007.

Nwogugu E.I., *Family Law in Nigeria*, op.cit., p.386.

Nwogugu, E.I. op.cit, pp.397 – 398.

Onokan Margaret Chinyere, Op.Cit Page 342 Osamuede Efe Sophia Op.cit pp 22-23. Nwabueze B.O Nigeria land law (Nwamife Nigeria 1972) p.393.

Osamuede Efe Sophia OP.cit pp 27-28.

Published by Digital Commons @ American University Washington
College of Law, 2004 Op.cit Richardson, Abby Morrow.
"Women's Inheritance Rights in Africa: The Need to Integrate
Cultural Understanding and Legal Reform." Human Rights
Brief 11, no. 2 (2004): 19-22..

Quar'an Chp. 4 verse 14, see Professor Yakubu *"Property Inheritance
and Distribution of Estates under Customary Law"* in *Towards
A Restatement of Nigerian Customary Laws* op. cit. pp. 144 –
145.

Quran Chapter 4 verse 11.

Quran Chapter 4 verse 12.

Richardson, Abby Morrow. "Women's Inheritance Rights in Africa:
The Need to Integrate Cultural Understanding and Legal
Reform." Human Rights Brief 11, no. 2 (2004): 19-22.

Richardson, Abby Morrow. "Women's Inheritance Rights in Africa:
The Need to Integrate Cultural Understanding and Legal
Reform." Human Rights Brief 11, no. 2 (2004): 19-22.

S.N.C obi, Women's property and Succcession thereto in Modern Ibo
law (Eastern Nigeria).

Sec.42(1) of the 1999 Constitution of the federal Republic of Nigeria
CAP C 23 laws of Federation of Nigeria 2004.

Section 2 Wills Law of Lagos State. *CAP 2 Laws of Lagos State 2003*;
S.4 Wills Edict Oyo State *CAP 63 Laws of Oyo State of
Nigeria 1990*; S.5 Kaduna State Wills Edict *CAP 163 Laws of
Kaduna State of Nigeria 1991*; S.5 Kwara State Wills Edict
CAP 168 Laws of Kwara State of Nigeria 1994;

Section 32 Constitution of the Republic of Uganda 1995, Section 38
Constitution of the Republic of South Africa 1996.

Section 41(1) 199 Constutution Of the Federal Republic of Nigeria
Cap C 23 laws of federation of Nigeria 2004.

Section 41(1) and (2) Constitution

Section 49 provides in detail for devolution of real and personal
property on intestacy.

Section 69. The Matrimonial Causes Act, Cap. 220 Laws of the
Federation of Nigeria 1990, defines *"marriage"* for the
purposes of the application of the Act to exclude marriage
entered into according to Muslim rites or other customary
law.The court held in <u>*Ahmadi v. Nwosu,*</u> [1992] 5 N.W.L.R.
278, that the Married Women's Property Act 1882 (a statute of
general application in Nigeria) is inapplicable to marriages
contracted and governed by customary law.

Socioeconomic and legal right of women: the challenge Women Aid
Collective (WACOL) Nigeria 2006) pg 5. WACOL is a non-
governmental, non-profit making organization in Nigeria
which is gender conscious working towards gender equality.

The case of <u>*Zaidan v. Mohsons*</u> [1973] All N.L.R. 86 illustrates these
points.

The Charter is now part of our domestic law by virtue of its
incorporation –CAP 10 Laws of the Federation of Nigeria,
1990.

The Igiogbe controversies in the Bini Customary Law of succession: Judicial Review op.cit at page XI; Benin Native law and custom at a Glance (Gift-prints Associates Nigeria 2007).

The prohibition of infringement of widows and widowers fundamental right 2011. No 3 of Enugu state of Nigeria law.

The Selected Judgment of the Lagos State Independent Shariah Panel Vol. I (Published by graphix solutions suite Nigeria 2005).

The States are Anambra and Enugu States – two of the Igbo speaking states.

These States are Western and Mid-Western States: Lagos, Oyo, Ogun, Ondo, Osun, Ekiti, Edo and Delta.

Towards a Restatement of Nigerian Customary Laws, published by the Federal Ministry of Justice, Lagos, Nigeria, 1991, p. 136. Nwogugu, E.I. *Family Law in Nigeria*, (Heinemann Educational Books Nigeria, 1990).

Ugbonna V Ibeneme (1967) F.N.L.R.251, Mojekwu V Mojekwu (1997) 7 NMLR (pt 215) p.283.

Wills Law of Lagos State *CAPW2 Laws of Lagos State of Nigeria 2003*; Wills Edict of Oyo State *CAP 63 Laws of Oyo State of Nigeria 1990*. Kaduna State Wills Edict. *CAP 163 Laws of Kaduna State of Nigeria 1991*. Kwara State Wills Edict. *CAP 168 Laws of Kwara State of Nigeria 1994,* Anambra State Administration and Succession (Estate of Deceased Persons) Law. *CAP4. Laws of Anambra State of Nigeria 1987.*